Laying Up TREASURES in HEAVEN

Alfred Prempeh-Dapaah

Copyright © 2018 by Alfred Prempeh-Dapaah.

All rights reserved. No part of this publication may be reproduced, distributed, or transmitted in any form or by any means, including photocopying, recording, or other electronic or mechanical methods, without the prior written permission of the author, except in the case of brief quotations embodied in critical reviews and certain other noncommercial uses permitted by copyright law.

Except otherwise stated, all scripture is taken from the King James Version of the Holy Bible (Public Domain)

Printed in the United States of America

ISBN: Paperback: 978-1-948172-94-3
            eBook: 978-1-948172-93-6

Library of Congress Control Number: 2018948760

Stonewall Press
363 Paladium Court
Owings Mills, MD 21117
www.stonewallpress.com
1-888-334-0980

Contents

CHAPTER ONE: THE HEAVENLY ACCOUNT 1
    Life and godliness 2
    Our divine inheritance 7
    Our spiritual or unseen blessings 10
    The promises of God 15
    The free and good gifts of God 19
    The fruits 23
    The treasures 26
    The Rewards 29

CHAPTER TWO: CHRIST, THE SOURCE 39
    A need for a heavenly vision in Christ 45
    Keep and maintain a heavenly vision 51
    Some truths we need to know 54
    The Holy Spirit reveals 55

CHAPTER THREE: THE HEART 63
    God, our sufficiency 70

CHAPTER FOUR: LAYING UP TREASURES IN HEAVEN 79
    What is a treasure? 79
    Laying up treasures 83
    The will of God 85
    The fear of God 88

    As unto the Lord 95
    Faithfulness 96
    Fruit bearing 101
    Evangelism 105
    Giving 108
    Giving to the poor 113
    Good works 114
    Sowing and reaping 117

CHAPTER FIVE: ACCESSING THE HEAVENLY ACCOUNTS 121

    Hearing the voice of the Lord 123
    Obeying the voice of the Lord 124
    Believing the word of the Lord 124
    Honouring the Lord 125
    Acting upon the word of the Lord 125
    Tithing unto the Lord 126
    Offering unto the Lord 126

CHAPTER SIX: LIVING UNDER OPEN HEAVENS . 129

    God's faithfulness 130
    In conclusion 134

CHAPTER ONE

THE HEAVENLY ACCOUNT

◇◇◇◇◇◇◇◇◇◇◇◇◇◇◇◇◇◇◇

> For the kingdom of heaven
> Is as a man traveling into a far country
> Who called his own servants
> And delivered unto them his goods...
> After a long time the lord of those servants
> Cometh and reckoneth with them
> Matthew 25:14, 19

> Therefore is the kingdom of heaven
> Likened unto a certain king
> Which will take account of his servants
> Matthew 18:23

> Not because I desire a gift
> But I desire fruit
> That may abound to your account
> Philippians 4:17

A heavenly account? Yes, a heavenly account; where your treasures are, and where your heart needs to be. There is an account for you in heaven in Christ, even as you live here on earth, which you may not know. But it is true. The moment you came into Christ, a heavenly account was opened on your behalf. This is a spiritual account but affects and influences one's life in the natural realm of life. It is divine and entails the totality of one's life, time, talents and resources in relations with their character and what they do with it here on earth, as far as the kingdom of God or the kingdom of heaven is concerned. The way one thinks, the way one speaks, one's ways of actions and reactions to the situations and circumstances in life and one's works or deeds; all go to account for him or her in this heavenly account. Whatever a person manifests, and whatever a person demonstrates good or bad; creates an occasion and opens doors, for something to be accounted unto him or her by other people (2 Timothy 4:16). These can be testimonies or a witness concerning you; in words, deeds or actions. Well, these accounts are accredited to you in your heavenly accounts. It also involves our lives on earth here in relations to with all what we do with our time, talents and resources; and how it brings glory unto God.

In this heavenly account, you, by the way you live in the kingdom of heaven on earth here, can lay up treasures; and from this account, you, by the way you live in the kingdom of heaven on earth here, can as well make withdrawals to meet every need of your life. And this is not to meet your needs only; but also to meet the needs of others as well; be it a spiritual need or a physical need. Be it a mental need or an emotional need. It is all possible with God; who himself is the creator of this heavenly account on our behalf through his only begotten and beloved Son Jesus Christ; by whom also he gives all things to supply and meet all our needs. Amen! Life in the kingdom of God here on earth simply means life as a Christian or life in Christ.

There are many things that this heavenly account holds for us but which we can perhaps not be able to talk about all in this little book. However, they include some of the following.

LIFE AND GODLINESS

This account holds for us, everything and all things that pertain to life and godliness for the believer in Christ. In other words, it contains and consists of everything of spiritual and material blessing that can help the believer to live a heavenly, divine or godly life in its abundant, maximum and exceeding overflow right here on earth, to the Father's glory. Hallelujah! And all of these are because of God's divine power which is in the believer. This is how the apostle Peter describes it;

> According as his divine power hath given unto us
> All things that pertain unto life and godliness
> Through the knowledge of him
> That hath called us to glory and virtue
> 2 Peter 1:3-4

From the scripture above, it is revealed to us that, the all things that pertain to life and godliness given to us are because of God's divine power. Now, this divine power is not outside of us. In fact, it is resident in us through the Holy Spirit. We should be able to have a revelation of this divine power which is resident in us, in order to learn how to live and walk in it. As we tap or live and walk in this divine power, we would also experience all those glorious things and blessings that pertain unto life and godliness. Again, this divine power is resident in us, all because of Christ, who as the power of God is resident in us (1 Corinthians 1:24). However, since it is God's own divine power, it is also worked out into manifestation and demonstration in us by the Spirit of God himself which is resident in us (Isaiah 59:19). As God works it into manifestation and demonstration; he directs it into all the things and areas that pertain to life and godliness for us to pursue them by faith. You see, this is how the bible reveals the resident of this power in us;

> For God, who commanded the light to shine out of darkness
> Hath shined in our hearts to give
> The light of the knowledge of the glory of God
> In the face of Jesus Christ
> But we have this treasure in earthenware vessels
> That the excellency of the power may be of God
> And not of us
> 2 Corinthians 4:6-7

So we learn from this scripture of how we have this treasure of the things that pertain to life and godliness in us; but that the excellence or the working aspect of this divine power to excel in life and in godliness is of God. For the bible says;

> For it is God which worketh in you
> Both to will and to do of his good pleasure
> Philippians 2:13
> (Isaiah 59:19)

Because it is God himself who works to direct his divine power which is resident in us, there should be a form of divine corporation with God; so that as he works this divine power into the manifestation and demonstration of all the things that pertain to life and godliness; we also would be able to pursue them by faith. And this form of Divine Corporation is made possible by the Holy Spirit of God who is also resident in us and connects us to the things of God (1 Corinthians 2:12). The importance of this divine connection is so that God can do greater things in and through us according to the pleasure of his will and unto his glory. This is how the word of God says it;

> Now unto him that is able to do exceeding abundantly
> Above all that we ask or think,
> According to the power that worketh in us
> Ephesians 3:20

By this same divine power resident in us, God works out to do exceeding abundantly above and possibly beyond all that we ask or think through prayer as we go about in our servitude or ministry in the kingdom of God. What we need to do is to learn how to depend on this divine power of God which is resident in us as far as all things that pertain to life and godliness are concerned. The apostle Paul testifying of this divine working power in his ministry; said in the following scriptures;

> Whereof I was made a minister according to
> The gift of the grace of God given unto me

> By the effectual working of his power
> Ephesians 3:7
> (Galatians 2:20)

And then again in talking about his preaching of the gospel to the Colossian church, he said;

> Whereunto I also labour,
> Striving according to his working
> Which worketh in me mightily
> Colossians 1:29
> (Zachariah 4:6)

In all things, it is by the power of God's might that we stand to be victorious as we live a godly life. The apostle Paul tells us;

> Finally, my brethren, be strong in the Lord
> and in the power of his might
> Ephesians 6:10

In whichever way this divine power of God in us is exercised in life, the good news is that, it is always purposed unto godliness or a godly life. That is, a life that manifests and demonstrates the image and character of God through Christ. It is a life that is manifested and demonstrated by the power of the Holy Spirit and the revealed truth of God's word. It is a lifestyle where God the Father inhabits mankind through his Son Jesus Christ and by his Holy Spirit. (1 Corinthians 3:16-17; 6:18-20). This is what the apostle Paul described as the mystery of godliness (1 Timothy 3:16) which he encouraged his spiritual son in the faith, Timothy to pursue as a young minister (1 Timothy 4:7). Not only that, he also encouraged him to teach doctrines which were according to godliness (1 Timothy 6:3). This was because the apostle Paul knew of a yet to come moment where there would be a form of godliness but without the power (2 Timothy 3:5). In other words, the teachings or doctrines would not be according to godliness.

Godliness is the lifestyle of the believer; and the encouragement of the apostle unto his spiritual son Timothy is good as well for the entire body of Christ in this present time, if not even more. The apostle Paul encouraged;

> I exhort you therefore, that,
> First of all, supplications, prayers, intercessions, and giving of thanks,
> Be made for all men; for kings, and for all that are in authority;
> That we may lead a quite and peaceable life
> In all godliness and honesty
> 1Timothy 2:1-2

> But refuse profane and old wives' fables
> And exercise thyself rather unto godliness
> For bodily exercise profiteth little
> But godliness is profitable unto all things
> Having promise of the life that now is
> And that which is to come
> 1Timothy 4:7-8

And to exercise oneself unto godliness is by the application of the revealed truth of God's word in one's personal daily life as a Christian (Titus 1:1; Hebrews 5:14). This is in order to benefit from the profits or blessings that go with the exercise of godliness. The apostle Paul revealed it also to us how we can live the life of godliness with contentment when he said;

> But godliness with contentment is great gain,
> for we brought nothing into this world, and it is certain
> We carry nothing out. And having food and raiment
> Let us be therewith content
> 1Timothy 6:6-8

The wonderful thing that makes godliness a great gain is the contentment that goes with it as a blessing. With God, it is not how much or how little you may think that you have; but how much you learn to depend on him to be content with what he blesses you with, be it great or small. The bible says;

> The little that a righteous man hath is better
> Than the riches of many wicked
> Psalm 37:16

And therefore again in Hebrews, it is written;

> Let your conversation be without covetousness
> and be content with such things as ye have
> For he hath said, I will never leave thee,
> Nor forsake thee
> Hebrews 13:5
> (Philippians 4:11-13; 2 Peter 3:11-12)

A basic foundation to live life and godliness with contentment is in knowing that the heavenly father is always there, and is faithfully ready to fulfill his promise to meet every bit of our needs according to the riches of his glory in his only begotten Son, Jesus Christ (Philippians 4:19)

So therefore, by living the life of godliness with contentment right here on earth; we gain and build unto our heavenly account in Christ.

OUR DIVINE INHERITANCE

This account holds for us, the reserve of all our heavenly and eternal inheritance in Christ. This is the inheritance unto which we have been called; and of which we have been made partakers in Christ. This is an inheritance which the bible says cannot be corrupted or is defiled; neither can it be faded away or be destroyed just as our Lord Jesus Christ revealed to us in Matthew 6:19-21. It is an everlasting inheritance of hope (Hebrews 6:19). All we need is to learn how to tap into them or walk in them by faith. We read in the first letter of the apostle Peter where it says;

> Blessed be the God and Father of our Lord Jesus Christ
> Which according to his abundant mercy
> Hath begotten us again unto a lively hope by
> The resurrection of Jesus Christ from the dead
> To an inheritance incorruptible and undefiled
> And that fadeth not away reserved for you in heaven
> 1 Peter 1:3-5

And then again, the apostle Paul adds the following scripture to show how believers in Christ have been made partakers of this heavenly inheritance in his letter to the church in Colossi;

> Giving thanks unto the Father
> Which have made us meet to be partakers of
> The inheritance of the saints in light
> Colossians 1:12

> Wherefore, holy brethren partakers of the heavenly calling
> Consider the Apostle and High Priest
> Of our profession, Jesus Christ
> Hebrews 3:1

How we receive our rewards of this divine inheritance from heaven depends on the activities or the motives of our hearts in terms of obedience towards the Lord and his word, since it is He who is the rewarder of our heavenly inheritance (Hebrews 11:6). It is in him, with him, by him and through him alone that we can receive the rewards of this heavenly inheritance; that is if we do all things in life as unto the Lord and not as unto men. Though we may be doing service to man, we should not think or see it as being done unto man but unto God. The reason being that God has made us as ministers of God and of Christ unto himself to serve others; and besides that, it is him that gives us the divine ability to do whatever we are able to do in order to prosper on this earth (Deuteronomy 8:18). The bible says;

> And whatsoever ye do, do it heartily as to the Lord
> Knowing that of the Lord ye shall receive
> The reward of the inheritance for ye serve the Lord Christ
> Colossians 3:23-24

> For this ye know that no whoremongers nor unclean person,
> Nor covetous man who is an idolater hath any
> Inheritance in the kingdom of Christ and of God
> Ephesians 5:5
> (Galatians 5:19-21)

The reward of the inheritance is also for them that are called in Christ. The bible says that "many are called but few are chosen" (Mathew 20:16). The good news however is that whoever is in Christ is also called of God (Romans 1:6; Galatians 1:6; Galatians 5:13; 1 Peter 2:9) and whoever is in Christ is also chosen of God (Ephesians 1:4; John 15:16; 1Peter 2:9) to be a vessel of honour according to his will and plan to serve his purpose in life. So whiles you count yourself worthy to be part of the many that are called, count yourself also worthy to be part of the few that are chosen. In other words live your life worthy by faith as one that is called, and live your life worthy by faith as one that is also chosen in Christ. This is the person who is well prepared and positioned in life to live by the eternal inheritance of God which is for him in Christ. In talking about Christ in relation with our heavenly inheritance, the word of God says;

> And for this cause he is the mediator of the New Testament
> That by means of death for the redemption of the transgressions
> that were under the first testament, they which are called
> Might receive the promise of eternal inheritance
> Hebrews 9:15
> (Romans 8:28)

However, the power or the attitude to receive the rewards of our heavenly inheritance rests on the practice and the exercise of the revealed truth of God's word in which we are to live and walk by faith and love. This is because, knowledge of the inheritance is made known only by the word of God and revealed to us by the Holy Spirit (1 Corinthians 2:9-12); but the manifestation of these inheritance in our lives depends on how we live and walk by faith and love. And also as a people which depends on the heavenly account or the kingdom inheritance. The apostle Paul in talking to the elders in the Ephesians church shared this with us and said;

> And now, brethren, I command you to God
> And to the word of his grace which is able to build you up
> And to give you an inheritance among all them which are sanctified
> Acts 20:32
> (Hebrews 5:13-14; Ephesians 5:5)

So here we see that the word of God does not only build us up in faith, it is also the key to acquiring an inheritance in the kingdom of God. Hence man shall not live by bread alone but by every word that proceeds out of the mouth of God (Matthew 4:4). For the entrance of God's word gives us enlightenment to have the eyes of our understanding open to know and enjoy the good things which God the Father has in store for us in Christ. As we practice the word of God and as we act upon the word of God by revelation for it to dwell and come alive in us, we gain a position in Christ whereby our inheritance are revealed and made known by the word which is come alive in us. It is call divine vision or insight.

OUR SPIRITUAL OR UNSEEN BLESSINGS

This heavenly account holds for us, all our spiritual blessings in the heavenly places which are in Christ. The bible says that;

> Blessed be the God and Father of our Lord Jesus Christ
> Who hath blessed us with all spiritual blessings in
> The heavenly places in Christ
> Ephesians 1:3

And these spiritual blessings are the unseen blessings which we, as a people of God's kingdom should live by, or are supposed to live by. They are as real as the material or temporal blessings. These are some of what I personally believe to be what the bible speaks of as neither eye having seen nor ears having heard; neither have they entered into the heart of man, the good things which God has prepared for them that love him (1 Corinthians 2:9). These are the unseen or spiritual good and perfect gifts which the bible says is from above; and comes down from the Father of lights, with whom is no variableness or a shadow of turning (James 1:17). The apostle Paul said something which may help throw some light on our lives as believers in connection with the unseen or spiritual blessings. He said;

> For our light affliction which is but for a moment
> Worketh for us a far more exceeding
> And eternal weight of glory
> While we look not at things which are seen
> But at the things which are not seen
> For the things which are seen are temporal
> But the things which are not seen are eternal
> 2 Corinthians 4:17-18

We shouldn't forget but remember that our inheritance is the eternal things that are not seen. It is good news to know that in the kingdom of heaven or of God on earth here, we do not live by the things that are seen (2 Corinthians 5:7; 10:7; John 7:24). Everything concerning our lives in God's kingdom is spiritual and therefore requires faith to access and enter to abide in them; hence the just shall live by faith (Hebrews 10:38-39). And because of these blessings in the heavenly places being spiritual and unseen, the bible says that, it takes the Holy Spirit of God to reveal them unto us (1 Corinthians 2:9- 10); and glory be to God, he has given us of his Spirit to reveal for us to know all and every good and perfect thing that are given us of God. This is how the bible reveals to throw some light on it;

> For what man knoweth the things of a man
> Save the spirit of a man which is in him?
> Even so the things of God knoweth no man
> But the Spirit of God
> Now we have received not the spirit of the world
> But the Spirit which is of God
> That we might know the things that are
> Freely given to us of God
> 1 Corinthians 2:11-12
> (Matthew 13:11; Philemon 1:6)

Our Lord Jesus Christ while he was on the earth said to us concerning the Spirit of God, or the Holy Spirit; who is also the Spirit of truth, how that when He comes, would be the one to reveal and show to us the things we have received or inherited of God.

> Howbeit when the Spirit of truth is come,
> He will guide you into all truth for he shall not speak of himself
> But whatsoever he shall hear that shall he speak;
> And he will shew you things to come
> He shall glorify me; for he shall receive
> Of mine and shall shew it unto you
> John 16:13-14

And if the Holy Spirit is going to reveal for us to know the things of God that are meant for us, he is going to do so from the inside of us where he dwells; not from the outside. And it is also going to be in line with the will and word of God; not outside of it. That is how God by his Spirit puts visions and dreams that need to be realized, in our spirits. And the moment the Holy Spirit reveals them unto us, we also come to know that it is ours to put in a claim or a demand for it. And not only do we place a demand for it by faith; we are also sure that we will receive it as we ask the Father in Jesus' name (John 14:14). The bible says;

> The secret things belong unto the Lord our God
> But those things which are revealed

> Belong unto us and to our children forever
> That we may do all the words of this law
> Deuteronomy 29:29

It is said that God reveals to redeem, but it should not be forgotten also that He reveals that we may do (James 1:22) or act on them by faith. You see, the faithfulness of the Father is such that, he will reveal for us to know that it is in his will and pleasure for us to have; so that as we go before him to ask for it, we go in before his throne by the boldness of the blood of Christ, and with the assurance of faith in our hearts, knowing that he will surely answer us, and that, we will receive it from him. Let us hear what the bible says in going before the throne to ask;

> Having therefore brethren, boldness to enter the holiest
> By the blood of Jesus, by a new and living way
> Which he has consecrated for us through the veil,
> That is to say his flesh; and having a high priest over
> The house of God
> Let us draw near with a true heart in full assurance of faith
> Having our hearts sprinkled from an evil conscience and
> Our bodies washed with pure water
> Let us hold fast the profession of our faith without wavering
> For he is faithful that promised
> Hebrews 10:19-23

And then again, we are encouraged by the word of God in the following scriptures to come boldly to ask and obtain from the Father;

> Seeing then that we have a great high priest
> That is passed into the heavens, Jesus the Son of God
> Let us hold fast our profession
> For we have not an high priest which cannot be touched
> by the feeling of our infirmities but was in all points
> Tempted as we are, yet without sin
> Let us therefore come boldly unto the throne of grace

That we may obtain mercy and find grace to help in time of need
Hebrews 4:14-16

And this is the confidence that we have in him
That if we ask anything according to his will, he heareth us
And if we know that he hear us
Whatsoever we ask, we know that we have the petitions
That we desired of him
1 John 5:14-15
(Hebrews 10:35-36)

There is a heavenly account with all the fullness and the overflow of the spiritual blessings that we have inherited; that we can claim and lay a hold unto it by faith in Jesus' name, amen! And these blessings, the bible says, are upon us to make us rich without sorrows in Christ (Proverbs 10:6, 22). However we as a people of God need to learn how to position ourselves to live and walk in the blessings of God by making the right choices and decisions with the help of the Holy Spirit. This is the way to have these blessings manifested right here on earth. Wrong and unguarded decision can and will deceive us out of God's will and plan in which we can have his blessings for us manifested. Jehovah the great I Am and God the Father says to us;

I have set before you life and death
Blessing and cursing
Therefore choose life (and blessing)
That both thou and thy seed may live
Deuteronomy 30:19

And since it is his desire for us to have life and have it more abundantly to live and be blessed in the overflow or riches of his glory; we should always learn to go for the choices that are in his will and plan, and that which would cause us to have life (Psalm 34:12-14; Proverbs 18:20-21) and be blessed (Psalm 1:1-3; Deuteronomy 30:15, 19; Malachi 3:10).

These spiritual blessings include all provisions that are paid for by the blood of Jesus Christ through the works of the cross of Calvary such as salvation, healing, deliverance, favour, prosperity, love, joy, peace, miracles, signs and wonders, etc, etc. They are just many.

THE PROMISES OF GOD

This heavenly account holds all the promises of God for us in Christ. These are promises laid down by the principles of God's word which means that, these promises are forever established in heaven, just as our spiritual blessings in the heavenly places are. Nothing can change it and they are as fresh as the very first moment that the Father pronounced them. The apostle Paul in his letter to the church in Corinth said;

> For the Son of God, Jesus Christ
> Who was preached among you by us
> Even by me and Silvanus and Timotheus
> Was not yea and nay, but in him was yea
> For all the promises of God in him are yea
> And in him Amen to the glory of God by us
> 2 Corinthians 1:20
> (Ephesians 3:6)

The promises of God that are yea and amen in Christ cannot be changed; and no man, not even the devil, can prevent or hinder the fulfillment of the Father's promises and blessings to come to pass and manifest in the believer's life in Christ (Genesis 1:27-28; Numbers 23:19-20; Hebrews 6:12- 18). They are forever settled and established by the word of God in heaven (Psalm 119:89; Isaiah 40:8; Matthew 5:18; 1Peter 1:24-25), or in the heavenly places where we are seated with Christ (Ephesians 2:6). However, it takes faith to be able to access them as and when the Spirit and the word of God reveal them to us (Romans 5:1-2). In other words, by faith we transfer, enter to abide dwell in the revelation of the word or promises of God for us and concerning us in and through prayer (Mark 11:24). It means that we have to release our faith to believe for them; and in believing for the promises and the things of God, it involves other things which include our personal attitude and response to the word and promise itself (Hebrews 10:35-36). One important thing is to count him faithful who has promised; no matter how the situation and circumstances might seem to be. By his faithfulness, God is exceedingly willing to answer us whenever we can rely and call upon Him (Psalm 143:1; Jeremiah 33:3). For the bible says that;

> God is not a man that he should lie
> Neither the son of man that he should repent
> Hath he said, and shall he not do it?
> Or hath he spoken, and shall he not make it good?
> Behold, I have received command to bless
> And he has blessed, and I cannot reverse it
> Numbers 23:19-20

Once God the Father speaks to promise, it is forever established. We should understand and be fully convinced by faith that, God in his truth and faithfulness cannot lie or go against his word and promise (Titus 1:2; Hebrews 6:17-18). It is rather we as his people that need to learn to count on his faithfulness which says that God is not slack concerning his promise, as some men count slackness (2 Peter 3:9); and hold on to the promises without wavering. And that we by faith and patience should believe and wait for their manifestation (James 1:6-7). For the bible says, he is faithful that has promised (Hebrews 10:23) which means that God has bound himself to his word of promise whereby he will not rest till it is manifested and fulfilled unto his glory. Why? Because he has decreed for his word not to return to him void till its purposes of blessings, favour and prosperity are accomplished into wherever he sends it (Isaiah 55:11), and again, he will watch over his sent word and hasten to perform for its manifestation and fulfillment of whichever situation he sends it into (Jeremiah 1:12) In talking about the promise of God to Abraham who is the father of us all as far as faith is concerned, we can learn more about the faithfulness of God also concerning his promise unto us. This is how the bible speaks concerning it;

> For when God made promise to Abraham
> Because he could swear by no greater, he swear by himself,
> saying, surely blessing I will bless thee and multiplying
> I will multiply thee
> And so after he had patiently endured, he obtained the promise.
> For men verily swear by the greater; and an oath for confirmation
> is to them an end of all strife
> Wherein God, willing more abundantly to shew unto
> the heirs of promise
> the immutability of his counsel, confirmed it by an oath;
> That by two immutable things, in which it was impossible
> for God to lie
> We might have a strong consolation, who have fled for refuge
> to lay hold upon the hope set before us
> Hebrews 6:13-18
> (1 Peter 1:3; Hebrews 6:19; Hebrews 12:1-2)

Here the bible reveals that Abraham endured patiently as he waited for the manifestation of God's promised word to him with an unshakable and unwavering faith (Romans 4:19-21). It is not that he didn't have faith, but in the course of releasing his faith to believe for the promise, the bible says that he endured patiently. This is one of the revelations and the mysteries of the kingdom of heaven which we need to understand about believing for the promises of God so that, when we release the faith of God in us to believe for his promises; we would also know and understand how to handle ourselves in the course of waiting for the answer.

This is because the release of God's faith in us also involves and goes with the knowledge of how to act upon or according to his will (Colossians 1:9; Hebrews 10:36), it involves endurance (Hebrews 6:15), it involves patience (Hebrews 6:15; 10:36; James 1:2-4), it involves perseverance (Ephesians 6:18), it involves confidence (Hebrews 10:35), it involves hope (Hebrews 6:12) and it involves trust (Proverbs 3:5-6) The apostle Paul by the word of God encourages us in a similar way, as we access the promises of the Father. He said;

> And we desire that every one of you do shew the same diligence
> To the full assurance of hope unto the end
> That ye be not slothful, but followers of them
> Who through faith and patience
> Inherit the promises
> Hebrews 6:12

So therefore there is the need for patience, as we also release our faith to believe for the promises of God; so that if we can understand this revelation in relations with how the Father in his own way works, and does everything according to the purpose of his will; we will also know and learn how to receive from him with expectation and joy. But not only patience alone, operating by the will of God also plays an important role in accessing the promise of God for us. Let us read for the record what the bible says;

> Cast not away therefore your confidence
> Which hath great recompense of reward
> For you have need of patience
> That after ye have done the will of God
> Ye might receive the promise
> Hebrews 10:35-36

As we endure patiently in expectation to see results concerning the promise of God, the bible says that we should not cast away or put away our confidence; while not forgetting to act according to the will of God. It means that, we should maintain our firm stands in believing concerning the promises of God, holding on to the profession or the confessions of the things that we have believed God for (2 Corinthians 4:13), and counting upon his faithfulness to answer us no matter how the situation or circumstance might be (Hebrews 10:23); and no matter how impossible the situation may appear to be (Matthew 19:26).

One of the ways by which we can keep our confidence is maintaining a stance of praise, worship and thanksgiving concerning the promises of God; remembering at all times the goodness of the Lord (Psalm 27:13). This helps us to glorify God and also build up our faith in a stronger way towards the manifestation and fulfillment of his promises. The bible gives the example of Abraham in the following scripture as he patiently endured for the manifestation of what God, who cannot lie, had promised him; and all was because Abraham counted Him (God) faithful;

> And being not weak in faith,
> he considered not his own body now dead
> When he was about an hundred years old
> Neither yet the deadness of Sarah's womb
> He staggered not at the promise of God through unbelief;
> But was strong in faith, giving glory to God
> And being fully persuaded that what he has promised,
> He was able also to perform
> Romans 4:19-21

One of the mysteries in counting on God's faithfulness is that, it transports us into the realm of a divine persuasion where doubt, worry, fear, unbelief, confusion and faithlessness about the promises of God lose their hold and control over our minds. It is therefore a wonderful news to know and learn how to count on the Father's faithfulness at all times; not only concerning his promises, but also his salvation, his deliverance, his healing, his blessings, his inheritance, his favour, his goodness, his grace and his mercies for us in Christ (1 Peter 4:19). Hallelujah and Amen!

THE FREE AND GOOD GIFTS OF GOD

This heavenly account holds for us, all and everything which God has freely given and continues to give for us to enjoy in Christ, even right here on earth both spiritual and material (Matthew 19:27-29). These include his grace and love; His salvation, healing and deliverance. The apostle Paul in his letter to the church in Rome spoke concerning how God through his Son shall give, and has given us all things freely to bless, favour and prosper for us to enjoy in him. Or better put, how he has by his Son given us all things freely to enjoy right here on earth. However, it is up to us to learn how to live and position ourselves in a way whereby we can enjoy these free things of God. Talking about God, the apostle Paul said;

>What shall we say to these things?
>If God be for us, who can be against us?
>He that spared not his own Son but delivered him up for us all
>How shall he not with him also freely give us all things?
>Romans 8:32
>(Matthew 10:7-8)

And truly, God has by Christ given us all things to enjoy in deed, for the bible says that the fullness of all things dwell in him (Colossians 1:16-19; 2:9). Not only are we given all things freely in Christ. We have also been given all these things to enjoy, and to enjoy them in their multiplication, in their increase, in their fullness, in their abundance and in their overflow in Christ (John 10:10). Hallelujah! And the glory is to the Father!!

Again in his letter to the church in Thessalonica, the apostle Paul encourages us;

>Charge them that are rich in this world that they be not
>high minded nor trust in uncertain riches
>But in the living God who giveth us all things to enjoy
>That they do good, that they be rich to good works
>Ready to distribute, willing to communicate;
>Laying up in store for themselves a good foundation
>Against the time to come
>That they may hold on to eternal life
>1Timothy 6:17-19

The bible says that for a person to be able to enjoy whatever is given him of God, is in itself a blessing from God the Father. There is nothing wrong according to the word of God to enjoy and rejoice in life on this earth by the good things of God, which he has in Christ for us. It is the will of the Father for us to rejoice and enjoy to the overflow to please and glorify him by all and everything that is good and perfect in Christ. It is his gift for us. It is part of his blessings and inheritance for us in the heavenly places. Hallelujah and Glory be to God! I even think it is a curse if one cannot enjoy from the good things for him in Christ. We are free and set at liberty to rejoice and enjoy in the Lord. Let us hear what the bible says to through some light on this;

> Behold that which I have seen
> It is good and comely for one to eat and drink
> And to enjoy the good of all his labour that he taketh
> Under the sun all the days of his life which God giveth him:
> For it is his portion
> Ecclesiastes 5:18

And then again the Preacher adds;

> Every man also to whom God hath given riches and wealth,
> And hath given him power to eat thereof and to take his portion,
> And to rejoice in his labour: This is the gift of God
> Ecclesiastes 5:19
> (Ecclesiastes 2:24-26; 3:12-13, 22; 8:15; 9:1, 7-10)

But however, many may not realize that this divine joy and the enjoyment of what we are given and blessed with of God, has much to do with being rich towards heaven (Luke 12:13-21) and giving cheerfully or distributing out of a willing and cheerful heart, the very same things which we know and believe that they are given freely unto us by the Father; whose will it is for us to give and bless others with what he has given us freely out of his love and grace. It is by doing this that the bible says "we lay up in store for ourselves a good foundation against the time to come". In other words, we lay up treasures to our accounts in heaven in order to be able to draw from in times of need. And not only that; but we also cause doors and windows of heaven to open and release blessings upon our lives as we give, share and distribute of what God gives us. Don't ever let us forget that God the Father always gives to bless us for a purpose which is to bless others; and to be rich towards the kingdom of God right here on earth. To be rich towards heaven or the kingdom of God simply means being committed to the church with one's personal life and the resources God has blessed him with on earth here. Let us not underestimate the power of the following scriptures and always remember the word of our Lord Jesus Christ unto us which says; "It is more blessed to give than to receive (Acts 20:35); and again ". . . Freely ye have received, freely give (Matthew 10:8; Acts 8:18-20). Therefore give and it shall be given unto you… (Luke 6:38)

And we should also remember what the apostle Paul said to encourage us with how we need to give in order to help lay treasures in our heavenly account. He said;

> Every man according as he purposeth in his heart,
> So let him give not grudgingly, or of necessity
> For God loveth a cheerful giver
> 2 Corinthians 9:7

It is after we have given, shared and distributed willingly in this manner out of our heart, that the bible says the Father makes all grace to abound unto our heavenly account to be used in times of need for what we need to do on this earth to lay up treasures in heaven (Hebrews 4:16). How he does it, we may not know or understand it; however we count on his faithfulness and release our faith to believe and trust confidently in him that it is so and that, it will come to pass for us to see the results. The word of God reveals it this way;

> And God is able to make all grace to abound toward you
> That ye always having all sufficiency in all things,
> May abound to every good work
> 2 Corinthians 9:8
> (Ephesians 2:10)

We should never forget but always remember and walk in the consciousness of the truth that it is never the will of God, our Father who is in heaven and of the kingdom in which we are, to be in lack, poverty or leanness; be it spiritual, material, emotional or mental. He has purposed for us to be full and overflow in his glorious abundance. All that he has for us and concerning us as far as everything he has given us as gift in his beloved Son Jesus Christ is concerned; is to bless, favour and prosper us even beyond our biggest imagination. Our God and Father do not do small things; just as he is great and big, so does he do all things and everything in his power. Don't forget but always remember that He is able to do exceeding abundantly above all that we ask or think according to the power that works in us (Ephesians 3:10) The bible says that our heavenly Father will not withhold any good thing from us (Psalm 84:11), but he will always give us good gifts (Matthew 7:11) and that every good gift, and every perfect gift is from above and comes down from the Father of lights, with whom is no variableness, neither shadow of turning (James 1:17). In other words, the gifts of God are irrevocable, without repentance or changes, as the apostle Paul says;

> For the gifts and calling of God
> Are without repentance
> Romans 11:29

This is in order that we come not behind in any gift (1 Corinthians 1:7). And the gifts of God includes salvation which is a package of his life, love, joy, peace, healing, deliverance, spiritual and material blessings to prosper and make us rich in Christ Jesus our Lord and unto the kingdom of heaven (Luke 12:20-21; Matthew 6:33).

THE FRUITS

This heavenly account holds for us rewards of all the fruits, the more fruits, and the much fruits we are to bear and would bear out of every good work we do in Christ. It is good news to know that in Christ, we are called, chosen, ordained, anointed and sent forth with the purpose of the gospel to bear fruit through evangelism and soul winning; some of which we may not personally be present to participate. However, through partnership in prayer and donations towards the kingdom of God through other ministries which are involved in soul winning, we become partakers of the grace that goes with evangelism and soul winning. The apostle Paul said concerning the believers in Philippi as they supported him in his mission works;

> Even as it is meet for me to think this of you all,
> Because I have you in my heart inasmuch as both in my bonds,
> And in the defense and confirmation of the gospel
> Ye are all partakers of my grace
> Philippians 1:7
> (Philippians 4:19)

Our Lord Jesus Christ taught us this in connection to fruit bearing;

> Ye have not chosen me but I have chosen you and ordained you
> That ye should go and bring forth fruit
> And that your fruit should remain:
> That whatsoever ye shall ask the Father in my name,
> He may give it you
> John 15:16

We are to bear fruit in the kingdom of God. God has made and purposed us to be fruitful and bear fruit in Christ. Fruit bearing is therefore an essential part of the believer's life in connection to laying up of treasures for ourselves in heaven. Even since ages and before the foundation of the earth, God in his own wisdom and the pleasure of his will had blessed us to be fruitful. It is as if God the Father created us just to bless for us to enjoy life in him. Immediately after the creation of man in his image and likeness according to the bible, the first thing God did was to speak and bless man to be fruitful.

And God blessed them, and God said unto them
Be fruitful and multiply
And replenish the earth and subdue it
And have dominion over the fish of the sea
And over the fowl of the air, and over
Every living thing that moveth upon the earth
Genesis 1:28

And again to Noah, God said;

Be fruitful and multiply and replenish the earth…
Bring forth abundantly in the earth
And multiply therein.
Genesis 9:1, 7
(Genesis 8:17)

The blessing to be fruitful and bear fruit in life is upon us in Christ (Proverbs 10:6). This shows that it is God's desire for us to bear fruit in Christ. Christ is the source of our fruit bearing. It is in him, with him, by him and through him alone that we can bear any fruit to the Glory of God. Our Lord and Saviour Jesus Christ said and revealed to us how important it is for us to bear fruit when he walked on the face of the earth over two thousand years ago. And not only that, he also thought us how important it is for us to acknowledge him as the only source by which and through whom we can bear the expected fruit unto the Father's glory. He said unto us;

I am the true vine
And my father is the husbandman
Every branch in me that beareth not fruit he taketh away
And every branch that beareth fruit he purgeth it that it may
Bring forth more fruit; abide in me and I in you
As the branch cannot bear fruit of itself except it abide in the vine,
No more can ye, except ye abide in me
I am the vine, ye are the branches, he that abideth in me, and I in him

> The same bringeth forth much fruit
> For without me ye can do nothing
> John 15:1-5

There are many other fruits in the kingdom of God or heaven that are there for us to bear unto our heavenly account; and fruit bearing is as important to God, as it is important for him to save us. Not only do we bear fruit to our heavenly accounts; but every fruit that we bear is and should also be unto God and his glory (Romans 7:4). There are evil and corrupt fruits (Matthew 12:33), just as there are good and pleasant fruits (Matthew 7:18-20; James 3:17; Solomon 7:13)
Fruit of righteousness (Philippians 1:11; Hebrews 12:11; Proverbs 11:30)

Fruit meet for repentance (Matthew 3:8)

Fruit of the Spirit (Galatians 5:22)

Fruit that abounds (Philippians 4:17)

Fruit of the womb (Genesis 30:2; Psalm 127:3; Luke 1:42)

Fruit of the lips (Isaiah 57:19)

Fruit of the ground (Genesis 4:3)

All these glorious fruits are there for us to bear in Christ. However in all, it is to the Father's glory.

THE TREASURES

The heavenly account holds all the treasures of God that are in Christ for us. And also, those ones which we lay up for ourselves in heaven are all credited to our heavenly account. Treasures are translated sometimes as rewards and crowns that we receive from God through the good works in Christ (Ephesians 2:10). Our Lord and Saviour Jesus Christ said and revealed to us that we can lay up treasures for ourselves in heaven. This is what he said;

> Lay not for yourselves treasures upon earth
> Where moth and rust doth corrupt and where
> thieves break through and steal
> But lay up for yourselves treasures in heaven,
> Where neither moth nor rust doth corrupt and where thieves do not
> Break through nor steal
> For where your heart is, there will your heart be also
> Matthew 6:19-21
> (John 10:10)

The treasures we lay up for ourselves are also the things that enable us to endure in life unto everlasting life. The things which credit our heavenly account involves the many things that also go to help us endure unto eternal life; both in thoughts, words, actions and deeds. In one other place, the Lord speaking to some of the disciples said concerning our endurance;

> Labour not for the meat which perisheth, but for that meat
> Which endureth unto everlasting life
> Which the Son of Man shall give unto you
> For him hath God the Father sealed
> John 6:27

The treasures we lay up for ourselves in heaven are sealed up among the treasures of God. God becomes the keeper of our treasures and he rebukes the devourer on our behalf concerning them. It is the more reason why I believe Jesus said no moth or rust can corrupt it and no thief can break in to steal because God himself is the keeper of it. He watches over it to multiply, to increase, to cause it to abound and to overflow. Not only that, but he also watches over to protect them from being broken into and stolen. And we should not allow ourselves either to be stolen from (John 10:10), but rather learn to keep them from being stolen (1 Timothy 6:20; 2 Timothy 1:14). The Father says it to us;

> Is not this laid up in store with me
> And sealed up among my treasures?
> Deuteronomy 32:34

God prophesied through the Prophet Isaiah that none can deliver out of his hand. In other words, there is no other power that can take away what God has and keeps in his hand, and that includes our treasures that are sealed among his own treasures. Our Lord and Saviour Jesus Christ put it this way when he talked about how secure God keeps them whom he has saved; which also includes everything concerning them (Psalm 134:8) and the treasures they lay up for themselves in heaven;

> My sheep hear my voice and I know them
> And they follow me and I give unto them eternal life
> And they shall never perish
> Neither shall any man pluck them out of my hand
> My Father which gave them me is greater than all
> And no man is able to pluck them
> Out of my Father's hand
> John 10:27-29

It is good to know that only God is able to keep these treasures and also open to release them upon our lives for us to enjoy them in Christ right here on earth as we faithfully live and walk in his word. The bible says;

> The Lord shall open unto thee his good treasure, the heaven
> To give the rain unto thy land in his season
> And to bless all the work of thine hand
> And thou shalt lend unto many nations
> And thou shalt not borrow
> Deuteronomy 28: 12

And the treasures out of the heavenly account is purposed to bring us into the overflow of God's blessings, favour and prosperity for our lives as his people in Christ (John 10:10; Ephesians 3:20). And by the release of these heavenly treasures of God the Father into our lives; we also by his grace are able to lay up treasures for ourselves in heaven. It becomes like a cycle of blessings, favour and prosperity; from heaven unto us, and from us unto heaven.

THE REWARDS

> Charge them that are rich in this world that they
> Be not high-minded nor trust in uncertain riches
> But in the living God who giveth us richly all things
> To enjoy that they do good, that they be rich
> In good works, ready to distribute, willing to communicate
> Laying up in store for themselves a good foundation against the time
> To come that they may lay hold on eternal life
> 1Timothy 6:17-19

The heavenly account also holds the rewards of the Father for us concerning every good work we do in Christ (Ephesians 2:10; Titus 2:14; Matthew 5:14- 16); especially when these good works are done willingly out of our hearts (1 Corinthians 9:17). Also, what makes these good works reward able is when they are mixed up with faith and love as we do them. You see the bible says that he who comes to the Father must believe that he is, and that he is a rewarder of them that diligently seek him (Hebrews 11:6; Hebrews 2:2); and truly, the Father rewards and this he does unto the heavenly account on our behalf (2 Timothy 4:14-16). Out of the same heavenly account, we receive from him the rewards of the good works which we do in Christ and in his name; in other words, what we do for the sake of his name as good works (Colossians 3:23-24). Our God and heavenly Father in his faithfulness is a rewader and he rewards our faithfulness in the things we do in his name.

The apostle Paul helps throw some more light on the questions we may have about our rewards in heaven concerning God's good works that are done in Christ. He said to Titus;

> And let ours also learn to maintain good works for
> Necessary uses that they be not unfruitful
> Titus 3:14

So therefore, good works are one of the means that make us fruitful unto our heavenly account. Some of the things done as good works in Christ and by which the Father rewards unto our heavenly account are revealed in the scriptures; some of which include the persecutions and sufferings we go through for the sake of Christ and his name. However, it is not that kind of persecution or suffering which a person chooses to afflict unto himself, thinking that he is doing it for the sake of Christ; but that which a person encounters and goes through, just because he or she lives and walks in the righteousness of God in faith and in love. The bible says;

> Blessed are they, which are persecuted for righteousness sake
> For theirs is the kingdom of heaven
> Matthew 5:10
> (Matthew 5:6; 1Timothy 6:11)

And as the Lord advices for us to first seek the kingdom of heaven and his righteousness and all things needed to live a godly life on earth here shall be added unto us, we should then prepare ourselves for moments of when we could possibly face and go through persecution (Matthew 6:33). It is just like the apostle Paul who experienced similar situations admonished us in his second letter to his spiritual son Timothy that "...All that will live godly in Christ Jesus shall suffer persecution (2 Timothy 3:12). This is because, as the apostle reveals in his letter to the Philippians church that it is given unto us as believers in the behalf of Christ, not only to believe on him but to suffer also for his sake (Philippians 1:29). But however hard it may be, the important thing is how well we will position ourselves during such periods where we allow Christ to become our focus (Hebrews 12:2) and also count on the faithfulness of the Father to see us through (1 Corinthians 10:13); as well as the rewards that are involved (Matthew 5:11-12).

> Blessed are you when men shall revile you
> And persecute you and shall say all manner of evil
> Against you falsely for my name sake
> Rejoice and be exceedingly glad for great is your reward in heaven
> For so persecuted they the prophets which were before you
> Matthew 5:11-12
> (2 Timothy 3:12; John 15:18-23)

The Lord has said unto us to remember that the servant is not greater than his Lord and that if he was persecuted, we also would be persecuted (John 15:20). The Lord's words stirs up the enduring faith of God in us to even rejoice and be glad to be persecuted for the sake of his name as his true disciples (Acts 5:41; 1 Peter 4:13-14), faithful ministers (1 Corinthians 4:1-2) and faithful ambassadors (2 Corinthians 5:20); knowing the glory it brings to God and the blessings and rewards that credits our heavenly account. The Lord made it clear unto us as his people about persecution in this life, and then assures us with these words;

> Verily I say unto you
> There is no man that hath left house
> Or brethren, or sisters, or father, or mother
> Or wife, or children, or lands for my sake
> And the gospel's
> But he shall receive an hundredfold
> Now in this time, houses, and brethren,
> And sisters, and mothers, and children
> And lands, with persecutions;
> And in the world to come
> Eternal life
> Mark 10:29-30

There is no way we should allow ourselves into being broken down because of persecution for being a disciple, a minister or an ambassador of Christ and our Lord. It is part of God's calling for us in his beloved Son whose sufferings the bible says, are examples he left for us to follow (1 Peter 2:21- 24). And just as our Lord was encouraged to go through the suffering of persecution by the joy he saw at the end, so should we also be encouraged by the end rewards, treasures and crowns of joy that are credited to our heavenly accounts to face and endure persecution (Hebrews 12:1-3). Don't forget, joy is also part of the contents in our heavenly accounts. This is what I personally believe and call as the righteous and fruitful sufferings in Christ as the bible says;

> But rejoice, in as much as ye are partakers of
> Christ's sufferings that when his glory shall be revealed
> Ye may be glad also with exceeding joy
> 1 Peter 4:13
> (2 Peter 1:4)

This is also a sign of actually manifesting and sharing in his suffering and glory as God's heirs and joint-heirs with Christ (Romans 8:17). Like the disciples when they were arrested and beating by the council for preaching, teaching and healing by the name of Jesus Christ, the bible says;

> And they departed from the presence of the council
> Rejoicing that they were counted worthy
> To suffer shame for his name
> Acts 5:41
> (Luke 21:33-36)

It is so amazing seeing some of the ways we could count ourselves worthy as Believers, but they are all a means of building up a better future unto eternal life. No wonder the apostle Paul boldly stated of how as believers in Christ, we need even to glory in tribulation knowing that tribulation works patience in us (Romans 5:3; 8:18; 2 Corinthians

4:17). And the bible says that it is in our patience that we possess our soul (Luke 21:19). After all, it is given unto us as Christians on behalf of Christ, not only to believe in him but to also suffer for his sake (Philippians 1:29) and that all who will live godly in Christ shall suffer persecution (2 Timothy 3:12); and therefore even have to bless and pray for them that despise and persecute us unto God's glory as the Lord teaches us;

> But I say unto you bless them that curse you
> Do good to them that hate you
> And pray for them which despitefully use you
> And persecute you that you may be the children of your
> Father which is in heaven…
> Matthew 5:44-45a

And then again the apostle Paul, who is known to have experienced much persecution and suffering for the sake of Christ, also puts it this way;

> Bless them that persecute you
> Bless and curse not
> Romans 12:14

It becomes quite understanding then that the apostle Paul, after he has had a revelation of the heavenly rewards, treasures and crowns that accompany being persecuted, afflicted and suffering for the sake of Christ and his name, was able to boldly declare and affirm with the following words of inspiration;

> We are troubled on every side yet not distressed
> We are perplexed but not in despair
> Persecuted but not forsaken
> Cast down but not destroyed
> Always bearing about in the body the dying of the Lord Jesus
> That the life also of Jesus might be made manifest in our body
> 2 Corinthians 4:8-11

I would personally not be surprised to believe that most of the persecutions and the sufferings we encounter for the sake of Christ are perhaps to help shape, reveal and bring out the nature of the indwelling Christ in us. Because as it is, Christ is not in us to be made a hidden treasure but to be manifested and revealed in and through us as the lighted candle on a candlestick (Matthew 5:14-16). Such joy of manifesting the Christ in us might be so great that the sufferings of these persecutions and afflictions for the sake of his name become light afflictions that are not even felt or noticed, as the apostle Paul reveals;

> For our light affliction which is but for a moment
> Worketh for us a far more exceeding and eternal weight
> Of glory while we look not at the things which are seen
> But at the things which are not seen, for the things that are seen
> Are temporal but the things which are not seen are eternal
> 2 Corinthians 4:17
> (Romans 8:17)

If we would understand the laying up of treasures for ourselves in heaven by God's perspective, and know that it involves every area of our lives; we would also see the many lots of ways whereby God directly and indirectly rewards our heavenly accounts. Not only are we rewarded for persecution, but also, being reproached for the name of Christ, there is a reward:

> If ye be reproached for the name of Christ
> Happy are ye, for the spirit of glory and of God
> Resteth upon you; on their part, he is evil spoken of
> But on your part he is glorified
> 1 Peter 4:14
> (Luke 4:18-19; Isaiah 60:1

Loving them that hate us by the love of God is also a means for the Father to reward our heavenly accounts. This is not the kind of love which is limited by the feelings of man. Because it is and perhaps shall always almost be difficult to love them that may hate us in the human sense of view. But when it comes to loving by the love of God, there is where the difference comes; and here, we are sharing light on the agape love of which God the Father is the source and giver of it. This love is so divine that its power is able to cut across barriers of race, creed and segregation to consume every form of hatred, jealousy and enmity. It is so strong that King Solomon in his songs described it as a vehement fire whose flames cannot even be quenched by any amount of water (Song of Solomon 8:7). Our Lord and Saviour Jesus Christ taught us with this scripture saying;

> But I say unto you, love your enemies,
> Bless them that curse you, do good to them that hate you
> And pray for them which despitefully use you
> That ye may be the children of your Father
> Which is in heaven... For if you love them which love you
> What rewards have ye? Do not even the publicans the same?
> Matthew 5:44-46

And surely, the only love by which a man can love them that hate him is the agape love of God. The bible says; for God so loved the world that he gave his only begotten Son, that whosoever believes in him should not perish but have everlasting life (John 3:16; 1 John 4:9). Now if we consider about what the bible says of how the world knows not God (John 17:25) and that the world hates God (1 John 3:13; John 17:14); we can then paraphrase John 3:16 as, for God so loved the world (them that hate and know him not) that he gave his only begotten Son (to them that hate and know him not) that whosoever believes in him should not perish but have everlasting life. This is truly the Love of God. It is a love that first takes the initiative to love, even if the fault is not from you (1 John 4:10, 19; Matthew 5:23-24). However, it is also a love that flows only through what I call as the channels of love; being a pure heart, a good conscience and an unfeigned or unwavering faith (1 Timothy 1:5)

Our Ministrations to the saints or the people of God in the love of God is also a means by which the Father rewards our heavenly accounts. Jesus taught us and said;

> He that receiveth a prophet in the name of a prophet
> Shall receive a prophet's reward
> And he that receiveth a righteous man
> In the name of a righteous man shall receive
> A righteous man's rewards
> Matthew 10:40-41

And which the apostle Paul also revealed through the following scripture;

> For God is not unrighteous to forget your work
> And labour of love which ye have shewed toward his name
> In that ye have ministered to the saints and do minister
> Hebrews 6:10
> (Colossians 3:23-24; 1 Thessalonians 1:3-4)

And in his reference to the ministration of good works unto him by the Philippians, the apostle Paul says of the Philippians;

> For even in Thessalonica
> Ye sent once and again unto my necessity
> Not because I desire a gift but I desire fruit
> That may abound to your account
> Philippians 4:16-17

Since it is more blessing to give than to receive, it is also good to consider the fruit that would abound to the giver's account in order to receive by grace. Our Lord Jesus Christ revealed that the Father is a rewarder of the good works which we do in and through his name. These rewards are also unto our heavenly accounts. This is how he said it;

> Take heed that ye do not your alms before men,
> To be seen of them otherwise ye have no reward
> Of your Father which is in heaven
> Therefore when thou doest thine alms do not sound
> Trumpets before thee as the hypocrites do in the synagogues
> And in the streets, that they may have glory of men.
> Verily I say unto you, they have their reward
> But when thou doest alms let not thy left hand know
> What thy right hand doeth that thine alms may be
> In secret and thy Father which seeth in secret himself
> Shall reward thee openly
> Matthew 6:1-4
> (Acts 9:36)

The Father rewards prayers prayed according to the right principles of his word (Matthew 6:5-13)

The Father rewards fasting that is done according to the right principles of his word (Matthew 6:16-18; Isaiah 58:4-12)

Surely, the bible says that there is a reward for the righteous (Psalm 58:11) and that everyman shall receive his own reward according to his own labour or good works (1 Corinthians 3:8; 1 Timothy 5:18; Psalm 62:12; Matthew 16:27).

However, it should be noted that one can lose his reward as the bible indicates through the teachings of our Lord Jesus Christ when he taught us and said;

> And whosoever shall give to drink unto
> One of these little ones a cup of cold water
> Only in the name of a disciple, verily I say unto you
> He shall in no wise lose his reward
> Matthew 10:42
> (Colossians 3:23-24)

And then again in talking to the Colossian church about the possibility of losing one's reward, the apostle Paul reveals concerning how one can be deprived of his reward through men. He said;

> Let no man beguile you of your reward in a
> Voluntary humility and worshipping of angels
> Intruding into those things which he has not seen,
> Vainly puffed up by his fleshly mind
> Colossians 2:18

Knowing that a person can lose his reward, I believe in what our Lord Jesus Christ said to the apostle John in the book of revelation to be very important; which we need to take note of and not fear any of the things which we would suffer for his sake (Revelation 2:10) but to hold fast that which we have so that no man takes away our crown or reward (Revelation 3:11). This is because of how our coming Lord and Saviour Jesus Christ has promised us concerning his future reward, treasure and crown for us;

> And behold, I come quickly and my reward
> Is with me to give every man
> According as his work shall be
> Revelation 22:12
> (Job 34:11; Proverbs 24:12; Jeremiah 17:10 & 32:19;
> Romans 2:6; 2 Corinthians 5:10; 1 Peter
> 1:17; Revelation 2:23)

CHAPTER TWO

CHRIST, THE SOURCE

This heavenly account, and all and everything which it holds and contains are in Christ, and so Christ becomes the source of it. He is the portal, the way, the gate, the door or the entrance into all what pertains to this heavenly or divine accounts. By him and through him, we access the contents of our heavenly accounts. When Christ is in you, the whole of heaven's resources are open up to you; which means that, one needs to have Christ in order to have and access this heavenly account. He is the way, and He is the key to access and draw from it in all its fullness (John1:16). It is in him, with him, by him and through him, that we can lay up treasures in heaven. And it is also in him, with him, through him and by him, that we can also withdraw and receive to have all our needs met from our heavenly account. (Philippians 4:19). No wonder when our Lord walked on the face of the earth over two thousand years ago, he declared to us about himself as;

> I am the way, the truth and the life
> No man cometh unto the Father but by me
> John 14:6

And then again in John chapter 10 he declares unto us;

> I am the door, by me if any man enters in
> He shall be saved, and shall go in and out and find pasture
> John 10:9

There are other things which are in this heavenly account, and these include the things which are already paid for by Christ; through his life, death, resurrection, ascension, and glorified position on the father's right hand side. These also include the things that his blood has purchased and established for all mankind; both believers and non-believers. They include salvation, healing and deliverance, peace, love, joy, blessings, favour, prosperity, abundance and overflow of both spiritual and material blessings. But as it is, one has a need of Christ in order to access them which comes by faith in him; hence the bible says;

> For God so loved the world that he gave
> His only begotten Son that whosoever believeth
> In him should not perish but have everlasting life
> For God sent not his Son into the world to condemn the world
> But that the world through him might be saved
> John 3:16-17

The word whosoever in this verse represents every person on the face of the earth; of every nation, every tribe and every tongue. That is everyone and anyone who wants to access these blessings of God through Jesus Christ; who is God's only begotten Son (John 3:16) and God's only beloved Son (Matthew 3:17; Matthew 17:5). It is in him that the fullness of all things is and consists; who also is the means by which a person can have access to them. The bible says;

> God, who at sundry times and in divers manners
> Spake in times past unto the father by the prophets
> Hath in these last days spoken unto us by his Son,
> Whom he hath appointed heir of all things,
> By whom also he made the worlds
> Hebrews 1:1-2

> For by him were all things created, that are in heaven
> And that are in earth visible and invisible
> Whether they be thrones, or dominions or principalities, or powers:
> All things were created by him and for him

> And he is before all things and by him all things consists
> And he is the head of the body, the church
> Who is the beginning, the first born from the dead that in all things
> He might have the preeminence for it pleased the Father
> That in him should all fullness dwell
> Colossians 1:16-19

> And of his fullness, have all we received
> And grace for grace
> John 1:16

The bible says that the Father loves the Son and has given all things into his hands (John 3:35). Not only that, but the Father also shows him all things (John 5:20). So when Christ Jesus came down on earth, he did not hesitate to reveal himself to the world about whom and what he is as the only mediator between God and man when he said; I am the way, the truth and the life and that no man can come to the Father except by and through him. As the bible says;

> For there is one God
> And one mediator between God and men
> The man Jesus Christ, who gave himself as
> Ransom for all to be testified in due time
> 1Timothy 2:5-6

Why? Because God the Father has delivered all things that pertains to life and godliness unto him (Matthew 11:27-28; John 3:35;) including all power in heaven, on earth and under the earth (Mathew 28:18; Philippians 2:8-11; Revelation 5:1-5); and that by him God supplies to meet all and every need of mankind in life (Philippians 4; 19; Romans 8:32). Again the Lord Jesus Christ said and revealed unto us that;

> For as the Father hath life in himself
> So hath he given to the Son to have life in himself
> John 5:26
> (1 John 5:11-12; john 17:2-3; John 5:21, 24)

So therefore, Christ Jesus in revealing one of his missions to the earth; which was to bring life in its truth and fullness unto the world and mankind said;

> ...I am come that they might have life
> And that they might have it more abundantly
> John 10:10

It is in the truth and the abundance of God's life which is in Christ Jesus that we are able to experience the fullness of all our blessings, the fullness of all our inheritance, the fullness of all our divine abundance and overflow and much, much more. They are all in Christ. It is of him, through him and from him that we have received of all things from God. Not only have we all received; but we all continue to receive from his fullness. And we will continue to receive of his fullness until he returns; because being the fullness of God, Jesus told us that he did not only come to give us life for us to have and just be satisfied; but he said he came to give it for us to have it more abundantly; meaning, beyond how much you can hold: Abundant life in the spirit, abundant life in the soul, abundant life in the mind, abundant life in body and abundant life in finances. This abundance is of a divine source where we come to a place of no lack, leanness or poverty (2 Corinthians 9:8) but a place where we live in a total provision and a continuous supply to meet all of our needs. It is good to know that, it is by this divine abundance and overflow that we also lay up for ourselves treasures in heaven (Matthew 6:19)

Though this fullness has been made available for all men; especially Christians, many are still yet to know how to live and walk in this divine abundance of the Father which are for us in Christ. In the first place being in Christ is something which is of a great transfer from lesser things into greater things. It is a divine transfer from the material into the spiritual from where we reign and rule to manage the natural things of life including our finances. It is to live life not only in the full but also in its increase, abundance and overflow where you become a blessing unto others and everything around you. You influence and radiate a life of success by the charisma of Christ's Spirit which is in you (Romans 8:9). What the church or the body of Christ needs is the spirit of revelation, understanding and wisdom to discern, live and walk in them to glorify the Father; while enjoying the full abundant and overflow of his blessings for us in Christ.

The apostle Paul who had this revelation about Christ as the source by which God is able to meet the need of every person, was bold to declare to the Philippians church after they had been a blessing to him in cash and kind during his mission works said;

> But my God shall supply all your need
> According to his riches in glory by Christ Jesus
> Philippians 4:19
> (Ephesians 3:20)

We should be bold also to declare "our God shall and will supply all our needs according to his riches in glory by Christ Jesus." Now the bible says that Christ is seated in the heavenly places, which are above all principality, power and dominion. From there he reigns and rules in glory, in power and in majesty. The apostle Paul in talking about how God raised and brought Christ to his present position which is above all principality, power and dominion describes it like this;

> Which he wrought in Christ when he raised him
> From the dead and set him at his own right hand
> in the heavenly places
> Far above all principality, and power, and might, and dominion,
> And every name that is named, not only in this world,
> But also in that which is to come
> Ephesians 1:20
> (Philippians 2:7-11)

At the same time, the bible says that God, the father, who is rich in mercy for his great love with which he has loved us; has also quickened or made us alive together with Christ, and has made us also to sit together with him in the heavenly places. It is good to know that all these heavenly places which are also in Christ, are the same places where the Father has made us to sit together with Christ (Ephesians 2:6). It is like we reign and rule with him from the same position, having made us kings and priests unto God the Father (Revelation 5:10). So we see that Christ is the source and the centre of all things that connects us to the heavenly places.

In other words, by being in Christ; we are in the heavenly places. So therefore; the heavenly places become an important issue for us; not only in word but also in reality. In reality means that, it is the heavenly places where we are seated with Christ in the spiritual realm that gives us our divine connection with heaven. The heavenly places therefore, have influence on our daily natural or physical human lives; and are involved with our daily activities right here on earth. However, the only means by which we can have this kind of divine connection with the heavenly places manifested and demonstrated in and through our lives is through prayer and the application of the word of God. Jesus taught us to commune with the Father in heaven and ask for his will to be done here on earth as it is exactly being done and established for us in heaven. Here the Lord gives us a revelation to open our understanding into how we are intimately connected on daily basis to heaven by our position in Christ; and therefore have to depend on heaven for our daily resources. In this case, we need to have and pursue a heavenly vision, even right here on earth in this life time. Not only the one to come when we would go be with the Lord. Hallelujah!

The fullness, the abundance and the overflow of eternal or everlasting life begin right from here on earth. We can live heaven on earth; and we are to live heaven on earth. That is the plan and will of the Father for us in making us to be seated in the heavenly places. Hence thy will be done on earth as it is in heaven. And for heaven's will to be done on earth means the manifestation and demonstration of God's will in and through the church; and that needs a heavenly vision.

A NEED FOR A HEAVENLY VISION IN CHRIST

The bible says that where there is no vision the people perish (Proverbs 29:18); and there are many things the word of God reveals for us to consider in building our faith and believing for a heavenly vision in Christ. These are the things that can keep us heavenly focused not in the afterlife, but right now in this life on earth here where we can live and walk with a heavenly conscience and in a heavenly perspective. This is where we as the body of Christ live every day with a heavenly awareness. It is good news to know that the heavenly places, out of where we draw our vision of heaven, are in Christ, and it is not just a fantasy or a kind of whimsical imagination where one cannot relate with. Though spiritual, it is as real and tangible as it is in the natural realm of life. As new creations in Christ, that is the place where God has made and purposed for us to live and sit as our present position in Christ (Ephesians 2:6). And having been made us to sit in the heavenly places in Christ, we need to learn and know what it is and how it is like to live in the heavenly places in relations with the present life on earth as Christians. This is what the bible says concerning the Christian and the heavenly places;

>Now therefore ye are no more strangers and foreigners
>But fellow citizens with the saints
>And of the household of God
>Ephesians 2:19

As fellow citizens and saints of God's household, we live and walk in the consciousness of heaven as our true home where we are involved with the activities going on there. And the apostle Paul in sharing light on our heavenly citizenship with the church in Philippi puts it like this;

>For our conversation (or citizenship) is in heaven
>From whence we also look for the Saviour
>The Lord Jesus Christ
>Philippians 3:20
>(Ephesians 2:6; Colossians 3:1, 3)

It is no wonder then, when the bible says of the early fathers of faith who for the sake of the heavenly vision they had, were not mindful of their country of origin but desired a better country which was or is a heavenly one (Hebrews 11:13-16). And again the bible goes on to make it clear as to where we are and have come to in connection with the heavenly places in Christ. Let us read in the book of Hebrews; this speaks to reveal and give us a little bit of knowledge about the heavenly places;

> But ye are come unto mount Zion and unto the city of
> The living God the heavenly Jerusalem, and to
> An innumerable company of angels
> To the general assembly and church of the firstborn
> Which are written in heaven and to God the judge of all
> And the spirits of just men made perfect
> And to Jesus the mediator of the new covenant
> And to the blood of sprinkling that speaketh better things
> Than that of Abel
> Hebrews 12:22-24

Here in the scripture above, the bible refers to the heavenly places as mount Zion, the city of the living God and the heavenly Jerusalem with a glimpse of an innumerable company of angels. If we can catch a revelation of what the bible is giving us now, we could as well understand the activities of heaven and that innumerable company of angels on behalf of the saints in the kingdom, and perhaps appropriate their beneficial purposes. The bible says that the angels are all ministering angels, sent forth to minister for them who shall be heirs of salvation (Hebrews 1:13-14). I believe it to be one of the main reasons why our Lord revealed it to us that we are in the world but not of the world (John 17:16). This is to get us rightly focused on our rightful place of citizenship which is of heaven; our position in the heavenly places on the Father's right hand side in him. In fact, the bible says of us Christians to also bear the image or the identity which is of heaven since we are citizens of heaven. This is how the apostle Paul said it;

> As is the earthy such are they also that are earthy
> And as is the heavenly such are they also that are heavenly
> And as we have borne the image of the earthy
> We shall also bear the image of the heavenly
> 1 Corinthians 15:48-49
> (Ephesians 4:22-24)

In other words, portray the characteristics of a heavenly being. And the image of the heavenly, is the same as of his Son Jesus Christ who came down from heaven (John 3:31-32; Romans 8:29; 2 Corinthians 3:18; Philippians 3:21; 1 John 3:2; Ephesians 4:24).

Now the bible says that just as he is so are we in this world (1 John 4:17) and therefore need not be conformed to this world in our own ways of thinking and acting (Romans 12:2); but by the spiritual mind of Christ which enables us to think and act like Christ (1 Corinthians 2:16; Philippians 2:5), we should transform our thinking and actions to be conformed into the image of Christ his Son (Romans 8:29; Ephesians 4:13).

How? By the Spirit of God who dwells in us and who also binds us in communion with the Father and the Son. This is the will, this is the plan and this is the purpose of God for us as far as his relationship with us in the heavenly places is concerned. You see, it was and still is the heart cry of Jesus Christ for us to be in unity with himself and with the Godhead.

In his prayer to the Father in John chapter 17, Jesus said;

> And the glory which thou gavest me, I have given them that
> They may be one even as we are one, I in them and thou in me
> That they may be perfect in one
> And that the world may know that thou hast sent me,
> And hast loved them as thou hast loved me
> Father I will that they also whom thou hast given me
> Be with me where I am, that they may behold my glory

> Which thou hast given me, for thou lovest me before the
> Foundation of the world
> O righteous Father, the world hath not known thee
> But I have known thee and these have known that thou hast sent me
> And I have declared unto them thy name and will declare it
> That the love wherewith thou hast loved me
> May be in them and I in them
> John 17:22-26
> (1 Corinthians 6:17; John 14:23; John 15:1-12; Romans 5:5)

The desire of our Lord Jesus Christ has always been for us to be wherever he is and might be (John 12:26; John 14:2-3; John 17:24; 1 Thessalonians 4:17); and his desire has always been to be wherever we as his people might be gathered together in his name (John 14:3, 18, 28; Matthew 28:20; Hebrews 13:5; Genesis 28:15; Matthew 18:20). And this also has to be our heavenly vision; to be where he is, united with him in the spirit (1 Corinthians 6:17) The church or the Body of Christ should have a longing, and an attitude of always desiring to be where our Lord is; that is in his very presence, the heavenly places. This is the purpose of the communion of the Holy Spirit where the body of Christ is bound together in a divine unity with the Godhead (2 Corinthians 13:14). However, this comes by keeping his word and acting by his word. We may have the knowledge of his word alright but if we don't keep it by walking in it, we may as well not be in the position to live and fulfill the life in the heavenly places which is in Christ; and where we are in divine communion with the Godhead. Therefore, as much as it is the desire of our Lord Jesus Christ to be in unity with the church, so must it be the divine desire of his church as well to be in unity with him who is the head of all things for the church (Ephesians 1:20-23).

Many may have the knowledge but the desire is not there. However, knowledge in itself is not enough to get us well positioned for the fulfillment of our heavenly vision. Knowledge should always be accompanied with a desire or what can be termed as zeal. They both work together hand in hand (Romans 10:1-2). Knowledge of the truth is the foundation upon which we build and grow after that we are saved (1Timothy 2:3-4; John 8:31-32; 3 John 1:2-3; 1 Peter 2:1-2). However, we must grow up from the knowledge realm of the truth we know into the revelation realm. It is within the revelation realm that divine visions and dreams, including that of the heavenly are received into our spirit. With knowledge come revelation, and with manifestation comes a demonstration of the heavenly vision. Jesus said concerning his willingness to be where we are and for us to be where he is;

> He that hath my commandments and keepeth them
> He it is that loveth me
> And he that loveth me shall be loved of my Father,
> And I will love him and will manifest myself to him
> John 14:21

And then again, he says to us;

> If a man loves me he will keep my words
> And my father will love him and we will come unto him
> And make our abode with him
> John 14:23
> (Revelation 3:20)

What we need to consider in the pursuing of our heavenly vision are that; in the heavenly places where we are in Christ and Christ is in us; we have been made to be:

Crucified with Christ, Dead with Christ, Buried with Christ and Resurrected with Christ unto a newness of life, where we live unto God and his will, but not unto ourselves;

> Know ye not that so many of us as were baptized
> Into Jesus Christ were baptized into his death
> Therefore we are buried with him by baptism into death
> That like as Christ was raised up from the dead by the glory

> Of the Father, even so we also should walk
> In newness of life
> Romans 6:3-4

We are also raised with Christ to be seated with Christ, where we are also glorified together with Christ. For this reason the apostle Paul encouraged us to hold on to our heavenly vision by setting all our affections unto the heavenly places where we are seated with Christ as he says;

> If ye be risen with Christ seek those things which are above
> Where Christ sitteth on the right hand of God
> Set your affections on things above not on things on the earth
> For ye are dead and your life is hid with Christ in God
> When Christ who is your life shall appear
> Then shall ye also appear with him in glory
> Colossians 3:1-4

So therefore in the heavenly places in Christ; we are dead to the flesh and its lusts and works. We are dead to sin and its lusts and works. We are dead to evil and its lusts and works. We are dead to the world and its cares and lusts. This means that, all these things unto which are dead in Christ, have no more power and dominion over our lives.

But praises be to the Lord; in the heavenly places we have been made alive in Christ to live unto God and his will (1 Peter 4:1-2). Amen! God has become our God just as we have become his people (Ezekiel 36:27-28; John 20:17); and God has become our Father (John 20:17) just as we have become his children (John 1:12; Romans 8:16). We can by faith and boldly declare him as our heavenly Father or our Father which is in heaven. He is our Abba Father, (Matthew 6:9; Galatians 4:6; Romans 8:15). Here, Christ's reference in giving us knowledge and revelation of God as our heavenly Father becomes clear to us (Mathew 5:45; 6:4, 6, 8, 9, 26, 32). We need to learn to know and relate to him and with him not only as God, but also as our God and as our Father (John 20:17) which is in heaven (Matthew 6:9, 26, 32).

The heavenly places in Christ are the places where God's presence abounds. It is where we live and walk in the Spirit and therefore are led by the Spirit of God as his children (Romans 8:14).

Besides, since the Lord has made us to understand that we are not of this world just as he also is not of this world (John 17:16), so also is the kingdom into which we have been delivered (Colossians 1:13), live and are to seek first (Matthew 6:33); not of this world. It is a kingdom that is from above, as our Lord Jesus Christ declared to Pilate in John 18:36. It is also the kingdom whose mysteries we have been given the divine knowledge to know and to know it for our good. The Lord in answer to a question by his disciples about why he spoke to the public in parables said unto them;

> Because it is given unto you to know the mysteries of
> The kingdom of heaven but to them it is not given
> Matthew 13:11

I believe it to be the more reason why the Lord encouraged us to seek first the kingdom of God and his righteousness. The more we seek for the kingdom or the royalty of God and his righteousness, the more the mysteries of the kingdom of heaven becomes known to us. The Lord said;

> But seek ye first the kingdom of God
> And his righteousness
> And all these things shall be added unto you
> Matthew 6:33

KEEP AND MAINTAIN A HEAVENLY VISION

The bible says that we have been made partakers of God's heavenly vision by his calling which is upon our lives in Christ (Hebrews 3:1-2); and as partakers of God's divine and heavenly vision, we need to learn how to keep and maintain it in order not to lose focus of it. The apostle Paul who knew and understood the importance of keeping this vision said he was not disobedient towards it. Disobedience can cause us to lose a focus of God's heavenly vision for our lives; and also his blessings for us (Isaiah 1:19). In talking to the king Agrippa, this is what the apostle said after receiving the heavenly vision;

> Whereupon, O King Agrippa, I was not disobedient
> Unto the heavenly vision
> Acts 26:19

One of the ways to keep and maintain a heavenly vision and awareness is through prayer. That is, prayer in the spirit. It is prayer in the spirit which plays the major role in our heavenly connection. There could be many other important roles that prayer in the spirit or tongues play, but I just want us to take a look at some few. While we pray in the spirit, it is the Holy Spirit of God himself that prays in and through us with words that cannot be uttered (Romans 8:26). Words that cannot be uttered are words that the human mind cannot comprehend or understand to explain. I personally have drawn a conclusion to call it a language of the heavenly places. I can now understand probably, why the apostle Paul called it tongues of angels (1 Corinthians 13:1). This shows how angels are involved with our prayers whenever we pray in tongues to communicate with the heavens. For the bible says;

> For he that speaketh in an unknown tongue
> Speaketh not unto men, but unto God
> For no man understandeth him
> Howbeit in the spirit he speaketh mysteries
> 1 Corinthians 14:2
> (Matthew 11:13)

In fact, the following scriptures may help throw some light on this prayer in the spirit; and the role the Holy Spirit plays.

But as it is written
Eye hath not seen, nor ear heard, neither has entered into
The heart of man the things which God hath prepared
For them that love him but God hath revealed them unto us
By his Spirit;
For the Spirit searcheth all things yea the deep things of God
1 Corinthians 2:9-10
(John 16:13-14)

Likewise the Spirit also helpeth with our infirmities:
For we know not what we should pray for as we ought
But the Spirit itself maketh intercession for us with groanings
Which cannot be uttered and he that searcheth the hearts knoweth
What is the mind of the Spirit because he maketh
Intercession for the saints according to the will of God
Romans 8; 26-27
(1 John 5:14-15; 1 John 3:21-24; Romans 8:1)

For he that speaketh in
An unknown tongue speaketh
Not unto men, but unto God
For no man understandeth him
Howbeit in the spirit he speaketh mysteries
1 Corinthians 14:2

We have been called in Christ to be reconciled with God the Father in a covenant relationship. And prayer, especially in the spirit, is the means to maintain this divine relation with God. Prayer builds and establishes our fellowship with the Godhead into an intimate communion with our heavenly Father. As we abide in prayer, communicating intimately with the Father by his Spirit that dwells in us, we maintain focus of his heavenly vision for us.

SOME TRUTHS WE NEED TO KNOW

Heaven is created by our Father (Genesis 1:1; Psalm 115:15)

Heaven belongs to our Father (Psalm 115:16)

It is the habitation of our Father (2 Chronicles 6:18)

Heaven is the throne of our Father (Acts 7:49)

Heaven is future home above (Hebrews 11:14-16)

We bear the heavenly image (1 Corinthians 15:49; Ephesians 4:24).

Our kingdom is of heaven (John 17:14; John 18:39; Matthew 6:33).

Our citizenship is of heaven (Philippians 3:20).

Our names are written in heaven (Luke 10:20; Isaiah 4:3; Hebrews 12:22-24

Our inheritance is reserved in heaven above (1 Peter 1:4).

Our spiritual blessings are in the heavenly places above (Ephesians 1:3).

We have been raised and made to sit with Christ in the heavenly places (Ephesians 2:6; Ephesians 1:20; Hebrews 12:22-24)

We have been made partakers of the heavenly calling and vision (Hebrews 3:1; Philippians 3:13-15) of which we are to obey (Acts 26:19)

All that pertains to life and godliness for us are from above (2 Peter1:3-4).

All that is giving for us to enjoy here on earth are from heaven above (1 Timothy 6:17).

All the good and the perfect gifts of the Father for us are from above (James 1:17; Philemon 1:6).

It is the more reason why our heart, mind and affections should be set on things above, where Christ, in whom and through whom all these things are and supplied is seated. And where, according to the word of God; we are also made to be seated in Christ. The apostle Paul encourages us in this way;

> If ye then be risen with Christ,
> Seek those things which are above
> Where Christ sitteth on the right hand of God
> Set your affection on things above, not on things on the earth.
> For ye are dead, and your life is hid with Christ in God.
> Colossians 3:1-3
> (Romans 6:3-5; Acts 17:28)

Surely, it is just like what the bible says; we live in the example and shadow of the heavenly things (Hebrews 8:5; 9:23-24) right here on earth by the spirit of revelation, who is the Holy Spirit (John 16:13; 1 Corinthians 2:9-12). It is him who leads and guides us in and through all the truth concerning the heavenly places where we are made partakers of Christ (Hebrews 3:14; 1 Corinthians 10:17; John 6:48-58; Matthew 26:26), His glory (1 Peter 5:1, 10; Romans 8:17; Colossians 1:27), His holiness (Hebrews 12:10). Most of all, we have been made partakers of the Holy Spirit (Hebrews 6:4)

THE HOLY SPIRIT REVEALS

The neither things which eye have not seen, nor ear heard and neither has entered into the heart of men (1 Corinthians 2:9), are all things that are in the spiritual realm or the heavenly places in Christ. But at the same time, these are the things which are normal for us to live by, or are supposed to live by if we understand the heavenly places very well. Again the apostle Paul by the inspiration of the Holy Spirit said in a scripture which throws some light on living by the unseen;

> For our light affliction
> Which is but for a moment, worketh for us
> A far more exceeding and eternal weight of glory
> While we look not at the things which are seen
> But at the things which are not seen:
> For the things which are seen are temporal,
> But the things which are not seen are eternal
> 2 Corinthians 4:17-18

And how are we able to look at the things that are not seen? Except by revelation of the Holy Spirit and faith; which the bible says is the substance of things hoped for and the evidence of things not seen (Hebrews 11:1). The Holy Spirit reveals but we by faith have to believe for them to come into manifestation by acting on the revelation of the word which we have received of the Lord. Faith is a fact, but faith is also an act. In other words, faith has to be put to work to see results of what we believe for. We believe to see by the faith of God (Psalm 27:13; Luke 1:45).

The Holy Spirit of God is him alone that knows the all things of God and can make them known unto us by revelation, so that we can know and live by the things that are not seen. In other words, the things that are not seen are made known unto us from heaven by God for us to live by them on this earth. The moment the Holy Spirit reveals these things that are not seen to us, then they become alive to us, and we come to know and understand that, they are meant for us to place a demand or ask to receive them through prayer. The revelation of the Holy Spirit comes by visions and dreams into our spirit with the word of God which serves as the seed of the unseen comes alive. In this way it becomes revealed and made known unto us. So that we can live and walk in the way whereby we can have it fulfilled in our lives.

> Now we have received, not the spirit
> Of the world, but the spirit which is of God
> That we might know the things that are freely
> Given to us of God
> 1 Corinthians 2:12
> (Matthew 13:11)

Unless the Lord reveals the unseen to us by his Spirit which dwells in us, there is no way any person will know the good things God has for us in his will, plans and purposes concerning our lives. And in the heavenly places, we live by the secret or the unseen things of the Father. The bible calls it the mysteries of the kingdom of heaven (Matthew 13:11). Mysteries are hidden truths; and hidden truths can only be made known by revelation of him who holds and knows them. It is the more reason why faith is so essential in order to believe for their manifestations in our lives (Hebrews 11:6). The bible says;

> The secret things belong unto the Lord our God
> But those things which are revealed belong unto us
> And to our children forever,
> That we may do all the words of this law
> Deuteronomy 29:29
> (Deuteronomy 5:29; Psalm 25:14; Amos 3:7; 1 Corinthians 2:12)

While God the Father will reveal them in order for us to know, we may not always understand them naturally (1 Corinthians 2:14). However by faith and through faith, we can understand and know them to be of good for us (Hebrews 11:3; Romans 8:28), knowing that our heavenly father will not give us anything bad or evil (Matthew 7:11). For the word of God says;

> Every good gift and every perfect gift is from above,
> and cometh down from the Father of lights
> With whom is no variableness
> Neither shadow of turning
> James 1:17

> For the Lord God is a Sun and Shield
> The Lord will give grace and glory
> No good thing will he withhold from them
> That walks uprightly
> Psalm 84:11

These are but few scriptures of the Father's promises that gives us the assurance of faith to boldly and surely declare that goodness and mercies shall follow us all the days of our lives (Psalm 23:6). And it is also because we know beyond the shadow of doubt that all that is of the Father will work for our good, as the bible says;

> And we know that all things work together for good
> To them that love God, to them who are the called
> According to his purpose
> Romans 8:28

And the amazing thing about the assurance of our faith and boldness concerning the revelations of the Father; is because he has already revealed the thoughts and intentions of his goodness towards us. The Father says to us through the prophet Jeremiah;

> For I know the thoughts that I think toward you
> Saith the Lord, thoughts of peace and not of evil,
> To give you an expected end
> Jeremiah 29:11
> (Isaiah 55:8; Psalm 139:17-18)

These are but a few of the scriptures that reveal and throw light on how connected we are with the heavenly places.

Then again, the bible reveals another important role of the Holy Spirit as the revelator in connection with the unseen;

> Likewise the Spirit also helpeth our infirmities
> For we know not what we should pray for as we ought

> but the Spirit himself maketh intercession for us with groanings
> Which cannot be uttered
> And he that searcheth the hearts knoweth what is the
> mind of the Spirit
> Because he maketh intercession for the saints according
> to the will of God
> And we know that all things work together for good
> to them that love God,
> To them who are the called according to his purpose
> Romans 8:26-28

The Holy Spirit of God praying through us by way of tongues is the fastest communication between heaven and us on the earth, as we abide in the heavenly places. We are actually talking to God as our Father without any interruption of the human mind.

> For he that speaketh in an unknown tongue
> speaketh not unto man but unto God
> For no man understandeth him
> Howbeit in the spirit he speaketh mysteries
> 1 Corinthians 14:2

Mysteries are a greater part of the heavenly places with which we are connected, and the kingdom of heaven in which we live; but prayer in the spirit plays an important role in revealing and unavailing them to us (John 16:13). No wonder the bible says that it has been given unto us to know the mysteries of the kingdom of heaven; or the heavenly places (Matthew 13:11)

And then again, prayer in the spirit builds, strengthens and sustains our faith concerning these things that are not yet seen in the heavenly places; but yet to be revealed and made known unto us by the Holy Spirit. These are the things that can be seen and acted upon only by faith.

> But ye, beloved, building up yourselves
> On you most holy faith, praying in the Holy Ghost

Jude 1:20

This kind of a prayer is that which seeks to know what the will of the Father in heaven is for us; and concerning us are, here on earth (Matthew 6:10). It is the kind of a prayer which we pray to seek and know what the thoughts and intentions of the Father in heaven for us are, especially here on earth (Jeremiah 29; 11-13). Again it is the kind of prayer that calls on the Father for him to reveal the things we need to know in order to live in the heavenly places on earth; while laying up treasures for ourselves in heaven. The Holy Ghost by inspiration, prophesied through the prophet Jeremiah and said;

> Thus saith the Lord the maker thereof,
> The Lord that formed it, to established it; the Lord is his name;
> Call unto me, and I will answer thee and shew thee
> Great and mighty things which thou knowest not
> Jeremiah 33:2-3
> (1 Corinthians 2:9-10, 12)

Being in the heavenly places also mean that, we have been translated from the power of darkness into the kingdom of his beloved Son (Colossians 1:13), and also into his marvelous light (1 Peter 2:9). Hallelujah!

This means that, we are in this world but not of this world (John17:14-16) and also that we are not earthy but heavenly and therefore, need to bear the image of the heavenly as well (1 Corinthians 15:48-50). To bear the heavenly image means that we have to put up attitudes that befit people who live in the heavenly places. And the image is that of his Son Jesus Christ (Romans 8:29). Jesus Christ is the image of the new man we are to put on (Ephesians 4:24). It is also because, our kingdom is not of this earth; but of heaven above as our Lord revealed to us in his answer to Pontius Pilate.

> Jesus answered; my kingdom is not of this world
> If my kingdom were of this world

> Then will my servants fight that I should not be delivered to the Jews
> But now is my kingdom not from hence
> John 18:36

Then again in his prayers to the Father, Christ reveals to us that we are also not of the world as he is also not of the world. If he is not of this world, his kingdom can as well not come from this world but heaven above. He said unto the Father;

> I have given them thy word and the world hath hated them
> Because they are not of the world even as I am not of the world
> I pray not that thou shouldest take them out of the world,
> But that thou shouldest keep them from evil
> They are not of the world, even as I am not of the world
> John 17:14-16

It means that we are in the kingdom of God and should learn to live by the principles of the heavenly places or God's kingdom right here on earth, where God's word teaches us that we should set our minds and affections on things that are above; where Christ is seated on the right hand side of the Father; and where the bible reveals that, we are also seated with him there. The apostle Paul said;

> If ye then be risen with Christ seek those things which are above
> Where Christ sitteth on the right hand of God
> Set your affection on things above
> Not on things on the earth
> Colossians 3:1-2

It is the more reason why I believe the Lord encouraged us to lay up treasures in heaven, where neither moth nor rust does corrupt, and where thieves do not break through nor steal; because there is where our hearts are; and there is where our hearts, as the children of God, are supposed to be, and should be (Matthew 6:20-21). Glory be to God and Amen.

CHAPTER THREE

THE HEART

The heart plays an important role in laying up treasures in heaven. You see, the born again heart is in the hands of God. Whoever is born-again has his new heart and life of salvation in the hands of God. It is God who actually directs every affair of the life and the heart in his children. The bible says that, the king's heart is in the hand of the Lord, and that, like the rivers of water, he turns it wherever he wishes (Proverbs 21:1; NKJ); and we should not forget that we are made kings and priests unto God in Christ (Revelation 5:10). This means that our hearts would be in God's hand, and He will turn it wherever He chooses. Again, the apostle Paul in encouraging the Thessalonians church concerning the love of God in connection with directing their heart said;

> And the Lord direct your hearts into the love of God
> And into the patient waiting for Christ
> 2 Thessalonians 3:5

As his children, God is in control of our hearts and therefore directs its affairs. This is purposely to please him, and to do according to his will. And also for God, it is the heart that matters (1 Samuel 16:7). It is his will that matters, and it is his pleasure that matters (Ephesians 1:11; Philippians 2:13)

When we are born again, we receive a new heart and a new spirit (Ezekiel 36:26). I personally believe it is these new heart and new spirit that actually gives us the identity of our new nature or creation. As we learn to live by the new heart and the new spirit based on God's word, we begin to manifest the life of the word as well by the power of the Holy Ghost in us. We change from the inside out into his image and likeness. Some people term it as metamorphosis. This is how the bible reveals it in the Apostle Paul's second letter to the Corinthian church;

> But we all with open face beholding as in a glass
> the glory of the Lord are changed into the same image
> From glory to glory even as by the Spirit of the Lord
> 2 Corinthians 3:18.

Functions of the new heart include its purposed to love (Matthew 22:37-39), believe (Romans 10:10) and trust confidently in the Lord (Proverbs 3:5) and in his word of promises without any doubt, unbelief, worry or fear.

It is a heart that is created and purposed to love by the love of God; which is an agape love. This is the kind of love by which he loved the world to give and sacrifice his only begotten and beloved Son for it. It is a kind of love which cuts across barriers; and pulls down strongholds of hatred, jealousy and bitterness; and it is the same God kind of love which is imparted into our heart by the Spirit of God who dwells in our hearts.

> And hope maketh not ashamed
> Because the love of God is shed abroad in our hearts
> By the Holy Ghost which is given unto us
> Romans 5:5

By this love, the Lord commands us to love him with all our spirit, soul, mind and body; and to love our neighbour as ourselves (Matthew 22:37-39)

By this love, we are to love one another in the body of Christ for the world to know that we are the Disciples of Christ. Jesus said;

Laying Up Treasures In Heaven

> A new commandment I give you that ye love one another
> As I have loved you that ye also love one another
> By this shall men know that ye are my disciples
> If ye love one to another
> John 13:34-35

It is this love that constrains us to love them that hate us and despitefully uses us (Matthew 5:49-46). It is a love so strong that it never fails, able to bear all things, believe all things, hopes for all things and endures all things because it suffers long (1 Corinthians 13:1-8). A love whose fire no water can quench (Song of Solomon 8:7)

The new heart is a heart that is created and made to believe by the faith of God, as our Lord Jesus Christ taught us in Mark chapter eleven verses twenty. This was a time with his disciples when Christ had demonstrated this faith of God against a fruitless tree by cursing it with the words of his mouth.

The following day as Jesus and his disciples passed by the cursed tree, and the apostle Peter drew the Lord's attention to what had happened; this is how the bible says the Lord answered him;

> And Jesus answering said unto them, have faith in God
> Mark 11:22

> For with the heart man believes unto righteousness,
> And with the mouth
> Confession is made unto salvation
> Romans 10:10

This faith of God does not doubt, and it is never afraid or fearful. Therefore again Jesus said concerning this faith of God;

> For verily I say unto you
> That whosoever shall say unto this mountain
> Be thou removed, and be thou cast into the sea

> And shall not doubt in his heart but shall believe that
> Those things which he saith shall come to pass,
> He shall have whatsoever he saith
> Mark 11:23

It is a heart that lives to trust confidently in the Lord despite situations and circumstances that seems to be above us. The bible says that we should trust in the Lord with all our heart and lean not unto our own understanding (Proverbs 3:5); for they that trust in the Lord with all their heart, not leaning upon their own understanding, shall be as mountain Zion, which cannot be removed, but abideth forever (Psalm 125:1)

Therefore it is God, by his Spirit in us, that directs our hearts and he directs it into his will, plans and purposes. If and when we can understand this very well, it will also help to build, strengthen and establish our faith in the Lord as well. The good news is that, no matter how the situation or the circumstance might seem to be; it is the will and desire of God to direct our hearts into all and every good and perfect things that he has for us in Christ and in his kingdom. It is his will and desire to direct our hearts into his love, his joy and his peace; just as it is his will to direct our hearts in the truths of his blessings, favour and prosperity.

It is also a heart that is made to reverentially fear the Lord in every area of our lives. Fearing God is the desire of God's heart concerning us as his people. He said concerning the Israelites to Moses;

> O, that there were such a heart in them
> That they would fear me and keep all
> My commandments always that it might be well
> With them and with their children for ever
> Deuteronomy 5:29

However, concerning the new covenant which God promised that it would not be like the former or the old one with the fathers, God promised to put his fear in the new heart he will give in establishing the new covenant. This is to enable us as his people the just, to live in reverential fear of him by faith. Through the prophet Jeremiah, God prophesied to reveal this when he said;

> And I will give them one heart, and one way
> That they may fear me forever for the good of them
> And of their children after them
> Jeremiah 32:39

Fearing the Lord with a reverential fear is something which is part of our blessings and inheritance in Christ. Not only that, but the blessings and inheritance seem to go beyond ourselves according to the prophecy through Jeremiah. It is also good unto our children that come afterwards. And what we should do is to learn and inculcate the fear of God into our daily lives. The preacher said in Ecclesiastes;

> Let us hear the conclusion of the whole matter
> Fear God, and keep his commandments
> For this is the whole duty of man
> Ecclesiastes 12:13

Fear God and keep his commandments also means simply; fear God and love him since keeping his commandment means loving him (1 John 5:3; John 14:15). In the New Testament, we are encouraged to live and walk in this reverential fear of the Lord. In talking about the fear of God, our Lord said to us;

> And fear not them which kill the body
> But are not able to kill the soul
> But rather fear him which is able
> To destroy both soul and body in hell
> Matthew 10:28

Our Lord Jesus Christ himself lived in the fear of God while he walked on the face of the earth. In talking about him, the bible says;

> Who in the days of his flesh,
> When he had offered up prayers and supplications
> With strong crying and tears unto him that was able
> To save him from death, and was heard
> In that he feared
> Hebrews 5:7

And the apostle Paul encourages us with many scriptures in his letters to the churches; but perhaps for the sake of space, we may not be able to include all in this book. However we will take a look at just some few with the following scriptures.

> Wherefore we receiving a kingdom that cannot be moved
> Let us have grace, whereby we may serve God
> Acceptably with reverence and godly fear
> For our God is a consuming fire
> Hebrews 12:28-29
> Let us therefore fear
> Lest a promise being left us of entering
> Into his rest, any of you should seem to come short
> Of it
> Hebrews 4:1

We should live by the fear of God in our servitude or ministry toward others. The apostle Paul continues;

> Servants, obey in all things
> Your masters according to the flesh
> Not with eye service, as men pleasers
> But in singleness of heart fearing God
> Colossians 3:22
> Servants, be obedient to them
> That are your masters according
> To the flesh with fear and trembling
> Ephesians 6:5
> (Philippians 2:12-13)

And concerning our salvation, the apostle Paul repeats;

> Wherefore, my beloved,
> As ye have always obeyed not as in my presence only
> But now much more in my absence
> Work out your own salvation with fear and trembling
> For it is God which worketh in you
> To both will and to do of his good pleasure
> Philippians 2:12-13
> (2Corinthians 7:15)

We are encouraged to submit ourselves to one another as the body of Christ in the fear of God; meaning that it takes the fear of God to be submissive in one's life. Submission therefore becomes one of the signs of the fear of God in a person's life. Not that we submit to man, but when you are able to submit to God, it becomes easier to submit one to another. And to sbmit to God in a reverential fear is to keep his commandments, which the bible says is not hard (1 John 5:3). The bible says it;

> Submitting yourselves
> One to another in the fear of God
> Ephesians 5:20

We are also encouraged to perfect holiness in the fear of God. Holiness is actually the reflection of the Holy God who dwells inside of us by His Spirit (1Corinthians 3:16). It then becomes important to know that holiness is not from the outside and therefore comes through some form of rituals; but it is rather from the inside out (2 Corinthians 3:18). It is one of the manifestations of the image and likeness of the God in us. The word of God says to us through the apostle Peter;

> But as he which hath called you is holy
> So be ye holy in all manner of conversation
> Because it is written, be ye holy, for I am holy
> 1 Peter 1:15-16

It is important to know how holiness is also attached to accessing the promises of God for us and concerning our lives. This is what the bible says;

> Having therefore these promises
> Dearly beloved, let us cleanse ourselves from
> All filthiness of the flesh and spirit
> Perfecting holiness in the fear of God
> 2 Corinthians 7:1

The reason being what I believe God spoke and prophesied through the prophet Obadiah when he said;

> But upon mountain Zion shall be deliverance
> And there shall be holiness
> And the house of Jacob shall possess
> Their possession
> Obadiah 1:17

GOD, OUR SUFFICIENCY

In the laying up of treasures in heaven, God becomes our sufficiency in all areas of life. Out of his glorious abundance, sufficiency and overflow, God the Father causes us to also abound in all areas of our lives. And the purpose is always the same as unto the good works of the kingdom of God (Ephesians 2:10). The bible says;

> And God is able to make all grace abound toward you
> That ye, always having all sufficiency in all things,
> May abound to every good work
> 2 Corinthians 9:8

And His name is El-Shaddai, the all sufficient God. He is a God who is more than enough and overflowing to give and bless beyond the human understanding. He lives by His name which is great and does all things in greatness; even exceeding abundantly above and beyond all that we ask or think (Ephesians 3:20). Therefore it should be known, acknowledged and believed that He is able to supply and meet every bit of our needs, so long as He is our God and we depend on Him. Our sufficiency is of God, so long as we live in His Kingdom. And this sufficiency goes also for all our spiritual, physical, mental, emotional and financial needs. It does not depend on anything which we can do, think or imagine apart from God. He has created us and he has made us; with everything that is within and without us. In the book of Psalms, the Psalmist declared;

> Know ye that the Lord he is God
> It is he that hath made us and not we ourselves
> We are his people and the sheep
> Of his pasture
> Psalm 100:3

We depend upon his Spirit for life; and it is his Spirit that gives us life. The bible says that He breathed into us the breath of life before we became living souls as we read in the book of Genesis and Job;

> And the Lord God made man of dust
> Of the ground, and breathed into his nostrils
> The breath of life and man became a living soul
> Genesis 2:7

But Job puts it this way;

> The Spirit of God hath made me
> And the breath of the Almighty
> Hath given me life
> Job 33:4

And the apostle Paul revealed it this way;

> But if the Spirit of Him that raised up Jesus from
> the dead dwell in you, he that raised up Christ from the dead
> Shall also quicken your mortal bodies
> By his Spirit that dwelleth in you
> Romans 8:11
> (1 Corinthians 6:18-20; Proverbs 18:14)

It is the same Spirit that gives us life that also empowers us to be whom and what God the Father has made us in Christ (Acts 1:8). Even the power to make wealth:

> But thou shalt remember the Lord thy God;
> For it is he that giveth thee power to make wealth
> That he may establish his covenant
> Which he sware unto thy fathers as it is this day
> Deuteronomy 8:18

The power to become His children;

> But as many as received him
> To them gave he power to become the sons
> Of God, even to them that believe on his name
> John 1:12

The power to excel in life over the enemy, the flesh, sin and the world; as the Lord said unto us;

> Behold I give you power
> To tread on serpents and scorpions
> And over all the power of the enemy
> And nothing shall by any means hurt you
> Luke 10:19
> (Matthew 10:1)

The power over sin;

> Let not sin therefore reign in your mortal body
> That ye should obey it in the lusts thereof
> For sin shall not have dominion over you,
> For ye are not under the law but under grace
> Romans 6:12, 14

Power over the flesh;

> This I say then, walk in the Spirit
> And ye shall not fulfill the lust of the flesh…
> But if ye be led of the Spirit
> Ye are not under the law
> Galatians 5:16, 18
> For if ye live after the flesh ye shall die
> But if ye through the Spirit do mortify the deeds
> Of the body ye shall live
> Romans 8:13
> (Matthew 26:41; Romans 8:1)

The power to be the witnesses of Jesus Christ;

> But ye shall receive power
> After that the Holy Ghost is come upon you
> And ye shall be witnesses unto me, both in Jerusalem and in all Judea
> And in Samaria, and unto the uttermost
> Part of the earth
> Acts 1:8

Not only by His Spirit are we made sufficiency of God; we are also made sufficiency of Him by his word. Having been born again by the incorruptible seed of His word (1 Peter 1:23); the bible says that we also grow by His word (1 Peter 2:2). Hence; man shall not live by bread alone but by every word that proceeds out of the mouth of God (Matthew 4:4). For the entrance of His word into our hearts gives light and brings enlightenment and understanding in every area of our lives (Psalm 119:105; 130); and the hearing of His word also brings unto us faith (Romans 10:17) by which we are to live (Romans 1:17) By his word, we receive life (John 6:63; 1 John 1:1) and by his word we walk in the truth for our prosperity and freedom (John 17:17; 3 John 1:2-3; John 8:32). We also depend on his word for our healing and deliverance (Psalm 107:20). The Lord says to us concerning his word;

> Heaven and earth shall pass away
> But my words shall not pass away
> Matthew 24:35
> (1 Peter 1:23-25)

And the again through the prophet Isaiah, the Lord says concerning his word;

> So shall my word be
> That goeth forth out of my mouth
> It shall not return unto me void but it shall accomplish
> that which I please and it shall prosper in the thing
> Whereto I send it
> Isaiah 55:11

> Then said the Lord unto me
> Thou hast well seen for I will hasten my word
> To perform it
> Jeremiah 1:12

This is how the apostle Paul reveals and shares with us concerning God as our sufficiency;

> And such trusts have we through Christ to God-ward
> Not that we are sufficient of ourselves
> But our sufficiency is of God who hath made us
> able ministers of the New Testament; not of the letter,
> But of the spirit; for the letter killeth
> But the spirit giveth life
> 2 Corinthians 3:5-6

As we learn to live and depend on God by his Spirit and by his word as the source of our sufficiency, we also receive life and enlightenment in our personal lives. We therefore, need to learn how to believe and trust confidently in him for all things; instead of depending on man, situations and circumstances of life. It is written;

> Trust in the Lord with all thy heart
> And lean not unto thy own understanding
> In all your ways acknowledge him
> And he shall direct thy paths
> Proverbs 3:5-6
> (Psalm 37:5; Philippians 4:4-7; Psalm 62:8; Psalm 119:133)

It takes only the heart of a person to believe and trust confidently in a person. But for us as believers and children of God especially; it is in God our father that we should trust with all our heart. King David, a man God said is after his heart, understood the need to trust in God. He exclaimed;

> In God have I put my trust
> I will not be afraid what man can do unto me
> Psalm 56:11

And trusting confidently in the Lord with all our heart, gives strength to our faith and love. It brings us into the place of his peace and rest without any fear whatsoever. Hallelujah! The bible says this in the book of Isaiah;

> Thou wilt keep him in perfect peace whose mind
> Is stayed on thee because he trusteth in thee
> Trust in the Lord for ever for in the Lord JEHOVAH is
> Everlasting strength
> Isaiah 26:3-4.
> (Psalm 37:40; Psalm 121:1)

So when in Matthew 6:33, God said we should seek first the Kingdom of heaven and his righteousness, I believe he was actually revealing to us, how we are to depend upon him, with all our hearts directed to where he desires and has purposed it to be; which is in the heavenly places. Unless we seek to find first the kingdom of heaven and his righteousness, we cannot know what we have, stored and reserved there for us as our blessings, inheritance and promises to withdraw from (1 Corinthians 2:9). Neither would we also know the kind of treasures we are to lay and how we are to lay them up there; nor would we know where our hearts actually are and supposed to be.

However, it is good to know that, the heavenly places are where our heavenly riches and glorious treasures are; and therefore also where our hearts need to be. Perhaps better put; where God's riches in glory and heavenly treasures for us are kept and reserved. (1 Peter 1:4). From there also in the heavenly places, the bible says;

> The Lord shall open unto thee his good treasure, the heaven
> To give the rain unto thy land in his season
> And to bless all the work of thy hands
> And thou shalt lend unto many nations
> And thou shalt not borrow
> Deuteronomy 28:12

Now, we have already seen how God, has made us to sit with Christ in the heavenly places, which means, we are not of this world and therefore do not have to be conformed to this world and its systems of laying up treasures or investments (John 17:14-16; Romans 12:2). This is not to say that it is wrong to lay up treasures or invest on earth; because the bible says that, a good man leaves inheritance to his children's children; and the wealth of the wicked or sinner is laid up for the just (Proverbs 13:22).

Our Lord also spoke to us concerning investment with his parables concerning the talents in Matthew chapter 25 and the rich man whose land brought forth an increase in Luke 12:15-21. While he was giving us a revelation on how to invest with our talents and gifts in the kingdom of God or heaven; he was at the same time pointing to us, how we should be rich and give towards heaven (Luke 12:21).

Furthermore, the bible says that we should be rich towards God and heaven; and this is what this entire book; laying up treasures in heaven is all about. It means that we don't have to live by the systems and principles of this world to be rich and lay up treasures; as far as the kingdom of God and of heaven is concerned here on earth (1 John 2:17). It is also not God's plan and purpose for us as his children, either to depend on the worldly resources. Rather, God the Father expects us to rely and depend on him directly as our source. After all, the heavens and the earth with all that are in them belong to him and we are his heirs. The word of God reveals to us that;

> The earth is the Lord's and the fullness thereof
> The world and they that dwell therein
> Psalm 24:1
> (Psalm 22:27-28)

Just for us to know how that our connection with the heavenly places is real; we should perceive it from God's perspective; how God has made us to be born again from heaven above and how God has made us who and what we are in Christ as new creations (2 Corinthians 5:17; Ezekiel 36:26-28)

CHAPTER FOUR

LAYING UP TREASURES IN HEAVEN

As it is, laying up treasures for ourselves in heaven involves every bit of our lives and being in Christ in connection to all that God has made and provided for us in Christ Jesus; and how we put every one of them to use by faith and in love according to his will unto his glory. This is what causes the Father to reward and bless us in our heavenly account. But then what is a treasure in the eyes of the Father? And what is a treasure from the kingdom perspective?

WHAT IS A TREASURE?

Now that we know we have accounts in heaven, the bible shows that, we can as well layup treasures in our heavenly accounts (Matthew 6:19), and also tap into it to make withdrawals of whatever it contains and is deposit in it. But we are going to talk about laying up treasures first before we talk about its access or how we can position ourselves for withdrawal. However, we need to have a heavenly vision which comes by a revelation of how we are connected to the heavenly places through Jesus Christ our Lord. He is the portal or the door, the way or the place of entrance, an access for both in and out concerning our heavenly treasure. Therefore, one important aspect of laying up treasures in heaven is a relationship with Him who is the source of it all; Jesus Christ, without whom it is even impossible to have and operate a heavenly account. This relationship begins by first seeking to enter the kingdom of heaven first; then God's right ways of life, which are necessary and which leads to the laying up of treasures in heaven. This is where Jesus revealed that, a man has to be born again of water and of the Spirit (John 3:1- 5). Being born and receiving the Spirit of God makes us children (Romans 8:15-16) and members of the royal family of God's kingdom.

> Now therefore ye are no more
> Strangers and foreigners but fellow citizens with the saints
> And of the household of God
> Ephesians 2:19

Not only members of the royal family of the kingdom of God and heaven; we also become heirs of God and joint or co-heirs with Christ

> And if children, then heirs
> Heirs of God, and joint-heirs with Christ
> If so be that we suffer with him
> That we may be also glorified together
> Romans 8:17
> (Philippians 1:29; Colossians 3:3-4; 1 Peter 4:13-14)

So what is a treasure, and what is a treasure in the eyes of man and what is a treasure in the eyes of God or in the kingdom of God and of heaven? What may be seen as a treasure in the eyes of man might not be what God would see as a treasure. However with the word of God, we may be able to gain an ice tip of what is considered a treasure in the Kingdom of heaven and of God; so we can also know how to lay them up in heaven. A treasure is anything which can be adored by a person with such an intimacy of passion. It is something which is desired, and cherished by a person with all his or her heart. Something which cause one to want to give, or is willing to possibly give up all things for (Matthew 13:44-46). A thing that is considered a treasure has a place in the heart and the heart also has a place in it (Matthew 6:21). In other words we are more affectionate about it. It is also highly esteemed in a person's life. The bible says that when Christ was born and wise men from the east followed his star and came into Bethlehem; they opened up their treasures and presented the little Jesus Christ with gifts of high quality namely; gold, frankincense and myrrh (Matthew 2:11). It is good and high quality things that come out of one's treasure sack, and one's treasure sack is the heart. Jesus taught us this way;

> A good man out of the good treasure of the heart
> bringeth forth good things
> And an evil man out of the evil treasure
> Bringeth forth evil things
> Matthew 12:35

> Then said he unto them
> Therefore every scribe which is instructed unto
> the kingdom of heaven is like unto a man that is a householder
> Which bringeth forth out of his treasure things new and old
> Matthew 13:52

In other words the heart becomes the vessel of a person' treasure; and the contents of whatever is in a person's heart becomes a treasure to him or her. And whatever is brought out from it becomes a treasure. A treasure can be good or evil. A treasure can be spiritual or fleshly. A treasure can be heavenly or earthly. But all in all, the bible says in the book of Proverbs that there is a treasure to be desired and oil in the dwelling of the wise (Proverbs 21:20), and as a treasure it always has a connection with the heart. The Lord Jesus Christ taught us that where a person's treasure is, there is where a person's heart is or will also be (Matthew 6:21). A treasure therefore can also be described as anything that comes out of a person's heart; be it an action, words or deeds. Even a person or a people can be a treasure based on the affection we have for and towards them. The bible talks of how God spoke concerning the people of Israel to be chosen as a peculiar treasure unto him after he had miraculously delivered them from out of the Egyptians hands, if they would obey and walk in his commandments. God said unto the Israelites;

> Now therefore, if ye will obey my voice indeed
> And keep my covenant, then shall ye be a peculiar treasure
> Unto me above all people, for all the earth is mine
> And ye shall be unto me a kingdom of priests,
> And an holy nation
> Exodus 19:5-6
> (Deuteronomy 7:6; 1 Kings 8:53; Psalm 135:4; 1 Peter 2:9-10)

There is also the Lord's good treasure which he opens unto us from heaven above to bless us, as the bible reveals;

> The Lord shall open unto thee his good treasure, the heaven
> To give the rain unto thy land in his season
> And to bless all the work of thine hand
> And thou shalt lend unto many nations
> And thou shalt not borrow
> Deuteronomy 28:12

There are hidden treasures of wisdom and knowledge which are in Christ (Colossians 2:3) and which the bible says we need to search for (Proverbs 2:4-6).

There are treasures of wickedness which the bible says profit nothing (Proverbs 10:2; Psalm 49:6; Mark 10:24; Luke 12:20-21)

There are treasures of deception (Proverbs 21:6; 2 Peter 2:3)

Then again, the bible says that the fear of the Lord is his treasure (Isaiah 33:6). In other words, the divine enablement to fear the Lord is in itself a treasure for us and in us.

There could possibly be many more diverse treasures, but the important thing is which of these can be laid up as treasures in heaven?

However if a treasure can be well understood through God's perspective, treasures will mean and be everything that comes out of the heart through thoughts, deeds, actions and utterances. It will mean and be everything that is done in the name of our Lord and Savior Jesus Christ. It will mean and be everything that is done according to the will of the Father. It will mean and be everything that is done; not as unto man, but as unto the Lord. And it will mean and be everything that is done alone unto the Father's glory. For as the bible says; his is the kingdom, the power and the glory into which we are called, and in which we live.

Once a young man came to Jesus asking the kind of good thing he could do to have eternal life, and Jesus told him to keep the commandments of which the young man said he has been keeping ever since he was a child as if to impress Jesus. But when this young man couldn't impress the Lord anymore; Jesus spoke the truth directly for him to go sell all that he had and give to the poor so he would have treasure in heaven and come to follow him. But the bible says that when the young man heard Jesus say that to him; he went away sorrowfully because he was very rich (Matthew 19:16-22).

Here, the Lord reveals to us one of the many ways to lay up and have treasure in heaven; and also be able to draw from it as well. And this is to follow him and follow him with all our heart. That is, to follow him in a way where nothing of this world matters anymore; but our relationship with him. The Lord said to Peter one day when Peter had asked what they would receive for following him, having left all behind. This is what the Lord said in answer to him;

LAYING UP TREASURES

Laying up treasures gives a sense of stocking or piling up treasures with expectation to draw from whenever it becomes necessary. A close example is like saving some money in the bank whereby one can draw from when the need arises. So it is not like something which one is laying up with the intention of using it anyhow, when there is not the need for it; or when it is not necessary to withdraw from it. Moreover, treasures are the things and issues that matters to the heart. They are the things which are passionately stored in the heart of a person; and they are the things that are done and come out of a person's heart. It can be a thought, a word, an action or a deed. A treasure in short, is associated with the heart. The content of the heart determines the kind of treasure; and the kind of treasure reveals the contents of the heart. Again the Lord taught us:

> For where your treasure is
> There will your heart be also
> Matthew 6:21

It may not necessarily be the thing that is adorable and precious but it is more of how the heart is attached to that particular thing, gift or present that actually makes it a treasure.

Likewise, laying up treasures in heaven applies to piling up or stocking things of great value to us only to be drawn from when needed. However, it may not be the things we do or give to lay up the treasures in heaven, but I believe it is more of how much the heart is involved, that makes it a treasure before heaven's eyes. It is the heart, its contents and how it lives in relation to the treasure that matters to God.

It is interesting to know that every treasure laid up in this account, and every fruit born unto this account is credited to us. It implies that we are able to withdraw from it. Paul said to the Philippians church:

> Not because I desire a gift but I desire
> fruit that may abound to your account
> Philippians 4:17

Which account could the apostle Paul be talking about? Their heavenly or spiritual account was what I believe the apostle Paul was talking about. So how do we lay up treasures in heaven? And how does God reveal it in his word for us so we can know and do it right to obtain the right results? We have already seen that, one of the many ways to lay up treasures in heaven is following the Lord with all our hearts (Matthew 19:16-22). Now the heart plays the central role of a person's life in terms of his thoughts, words, actions and deeds. So in other words, laying up treasure for one's self involves whatever a person does with his or her life. It involves whatever a person owes as a gift, a talent, in cash and in kind. It involves a person's environment and especially in relationship with his Creator. The bible says that whatever a person sows in life, that shall he or she reap; be it spiritual, physical, mental or emotional (Galatians 6:6-7). And in whichever measure it is sown so also shall it be reaped or given back (2 Corinthians 9:6).

Whatever a person sets in his or her heart that is what that person will build a treasure unto. If we sow to the flesh we shall reap of the flesh. If we sow to the spirit we shall reap of the spirit. If we sow to love we shall reap of love. If we sow to peace we shall reap of peace. If we sow to the world we shall reap of the world or worldliness. If we sow to heaven we shall reap of heaven. If we sow to the earth we shall reap of the earth or earthy. However as believers, our Lord has taught us not to lay up treasures for ourselves upon the earth because moth and rust can corrupt them and thieves can break through and steal them (Matthew 6:19), neither should we lay up for ourselves treasures in the flesh (Galatians 5:13) nor in the world for the bible says that the world passes away with all the lusts that are in it (1 John 2:17). That will also include whatever treasures we may lay up in it for ourselves.

THE WILL OF GOD

One other way we can consider to laying up treasures in heaven, is by living and doing all things with the heart according to the will of God. In Christ, we live unto God as our heavenly Father and as our heavenly Father; we live also unto his will and according to his will. Seeing, he works all things in us by his spirit to will and to do for his pleasure. This is because our heavenly Father does all things according to the pleasure of his will (Ephesians 1:5, 11).

It is by his will that he has begotten us again in Christ as his children (John 1:12-13; 1 Peter 1:3, 23; James 1:18; 1 Corinthians 4:15). It is according to his will that we live as his children (1 Peter 4:2). It is his will which also qualifies us as his children (Matthew 12:49-50). It is by his will that we do all things in Christ (Matthew 7:21-22), and doing all things according to his will is also like doing all things as unto the Lord (Colossians 3:23).

The apostle Paul reveals to us in his letter to the Romans that we are supposed to live unto God just as Christ also did. In talking about Christ, he said;

> For in that he died, he died to sin once
> But in that he liveth, he liveth unto God
> Likewise, reckon ye also yourselves to be dead indeed
> Unto sin but alive unto God through Jesus Christ
> Our Lord
> Romans 6:11

But the apostle Peter also reveals that, not only are we to live unto God; but we are also to live unto and according to God's will just as Christ also did (John 6:38, Matthew 6:10), because he has also made us to be dead unto sin. In other words, if God has made us dead unto sin in Christ; there is no other way for us to live but unto his will and according to his will. This is how the apostle Peter puts it;

> Forasmuch then as Christ hath suffered for us in the flesh
> Arm yourselves likewise with the same mind
> For he that hath suffered in the flesh
> Hath ceased from sin that he no longer should live
> the rest of his time in the lusts of men, but to the will of God
> 1 Peter 4:1-2

Living unto the Lord and doing the will of God brings glory unto Him; and it is only the things done to bring glory to God our Father, which also rewards our heavenly account; especially when it is done with the heart. There is nothing that glorifies God than the things that are done with the heart and from the heart (Exodus 25:1-2). It was only after our Lord Jesus Christ had done the will of God that he could ask the Father to glorify him with himself (John 17:1)

The fulfillment of God's promises in our lives, which is also a form of withdrawal from our heavenly account, is tied to doing the will of the Father, the bible says;

> Cast not away therefore your confidence
> Which hath a great recompense of reward
> For ye have need of patience
> That after ye have done the will of God
> Ye might receive the promise
> Hebrews 10:35-36

Then again in the book of Matthew, the Lord boldly declares to us;

> Not everyone that saith unto me Lord, Lord,
> Shall enter into the kingdom of heaven
> But he that doeth the will of my Father
> Which is in heaven
> Matthew 7:21

And speaking unto the disciples concerning us as the children of God (John 1:13) and his true family, the Lord said;

> Behold my mother and my brethren
> For whosoever shall do the will of my Father
> Which is in heaven, the same is
> My brother, and sister, and mother
> Matthew 12:49-50

So therefore, doing the will of God our Father becomes an important factor in our lives as a people of God. It is also important unto us, as far as laying up treasures and withdrawing of our treasures in heaven is concerned. Hence;

> Our Father which art in heaven
> Hallowed be thy name
> Thy kingdom come, thy will be done in earth,
> As it is in heaven
> Matthew 6:10

THE FEAR OF GOD

Laying up treasures in heaven involves our reverence fear for God in all that we do in every area of our lives; especially when we are in Christ. Once again, let us remind ourselves that, whatever we do to lay up treasures in heaven, or do to credit our heavenly account; are not the things that we do as unto men, but they are things that we do as unto God our Father. They are things which we do as unto his will and according to his will. The Lord teaches us to take heed that we do not our alms and for that matter, anything and everything we do to lay up treasures for ourselves in heaven before men just to be seen of them; otherwise we have no reward of our Father in heaven (Matthew 6:1) This does not matter who or what the person might be. The bible says that God is not a respecter of persons, but that in every nation he that fears him and works righteousness is accepted with him (Acts 10:34-35). Therefore when we purpose in our lives to live unto the will of our Father which is in heaven, personalities does not count, only Christ matters as the apostle James, the brother of our Lord Jesus Christ stated it;

> My brethren,
> Have not the faith of our Lord Jesus Christ
> The Lord of glory with respect
> Of persons
> James 2:1

This is a sense of reverential fear unto our God and Father which is in heaven; who himself is also not a respecter of persons. So the apostle Paul reveals to us the importance of the reverential fear of God as citizens in the kingdom of God when he said;

> Wherefore we receiving a kingdom which
> Cannot be moved let us have grace whereby we may
> Serve God acceptably with reverence and godly fear
> For our God is a consuming fire
> Hebrews 12:28-29
> (Hebrews 4:16)

This reverential fear of God should become an integrated part of our lives that; we not only have to demonstrate it only when we do services unto God, but that also it is evidenced in our daily activities and duties unto men as well. It is a sign of submission unto God. This is because we do what we do based on the word and the will of God. Every time we do anything based on the motivation of God's word and his will, we are submitting to him and his authority, although what we would be doing is actually for men and unto men. The apostle Paul encouraging the born again slaves in the church of the Colossians concerning the fear of God said;

> Servants, obey in all things
> Your masters according to the flesh
> Not with eye service as men pleasers
> But in singleness of heart; fearing God
> Colossians 3:22

And our submission unto the Lord also becomes a reflection in our relations with one another in the body of Christ, which is also motivated by the fear of God. Here again, the apostle Paul encourages us;

> Giving thanks always for all things
> Unto God and the Father in the name of our Lord Jesus Christ

> Submitting yourselves one to another
> In the fear of God
> Ephesians 5:20-21

By the fear of God we submit ourselves one to anther in the body of Christ. Many a people in the house of God are not able to submit unto one another because they are not walking in the fear of God. These are some of the various things that contribute to building up credits of blessings unto our heavenly accounts. Therefore also, the inability to submit to one another especially in the house of God, blocks most of the divine and heavenly blessings from being released into their lives. Many may not be aware but submission in itself is a form of giving and sowing which bring returns as we learn to walk in it. Not walking in the fear of God also defiles us. In other words, the word of God reveals how holiness is perfected in our lives at the same time that we live and walk in the fear of God. This is what the word of God says through the apostle Paul;

> Having therefore these promises,
> Dearly beloved, let us cleanse ourselves
> From all filthiness of the flesh and spirit
> Perfecting holiness in the fear of God
> 2 Corinthians 7:1
> (2 Corinthians 1:20)

In the book of Ecclesiastes, the preacher in his last sermon draws our attention to what is actually the whole duty of man and especially the believer; which includes the fear of God. Let us hear the Preacher's own words;

> Let us hear the conclusion of the whole matter
> Fear God and keep his commandments
> For this is the whole duty of man
> Ecclesiastes 12:13

What kind of duty does the bible talks about? There may be many other explanations but I believe this whole duty of man includes the very many plans and purposes of God ordained for us in Christ to live and walk in them by faith and love; which also abound, account and contribute to the laying up of treasures for ourselves in heaven. For the bible says;

> For God shall bring every work into judgment,
> with every secret thing, whether it be good or bad
> Ecclesiastes 12:14

Then the apostle Paul also said this to remind us of God's faithfulness to reward every good work unto which we have been predestinated by God in Christ; the bible says;

> For we are his workmanship created in Christ Jesus
> unto good works which God hath before ordained
> That we should walk in them
> Ephesians 2:10

These ordained or prepared good works are those which are purposed of God according to the pleasure of his will. They are therefore done in the will of God by faith and in love. These are also works that are rewarded of God and accounts to our heavenly credits or blessings in Christ and in the heavenly places. And the faithfulness of God is as the word of God says;

> For God is not unrighteous to forget your work
> And labour of love which ye have shown
> Toward his name in that ye have ministered to
> the saints and do minister
> Hebrews 6:10
> (Hebrews 11:6)

It is therefore important as a people of God to learn how to let the fear of God become the motivational factor in all that we do; unto God and unto man which only takes the heart. For where your treasure is, there will your heart also be (Matthew 6:21); and our treasure is in heaven and there is where our heart and our affections also should be as well (Colossians 3:2).

One may perhaps ask what the fear of God could have in relations with the laying up of treasures in heaven; but it is good to know that a lot of blessings come with the fear of God which abounds unto our heavenly account. Moreover, if we can understand that our blessings are kept and reserved in our heavenly account, waiting to be withdrawn and that fearing God is a means of positioning ourselves for the blessings; we would not underestimate serving the Lord with a fearful heart. However, there are many scriptures concerning these blessings that we can draw inspiration from; but we will only take some few. The bible says;

> Blessed is the man that walketh not in the counsel
> Of the ungodly, nor standeth in the way of sinners, nor sitteth
> In the seat of the scornful, but his delight is in
> The law of the Lord, and in his law
> Doth he meditate day and night
> Psalm 1:1-2
> (Joshua 1:8)

The above scripture reveals how we can position ourselves in Christ in order to access and manifest the many blessings of God that are laid down for us in Christ; which includes a delight in the word and commandments of God. The Psalmist declares;

> Praise ye the Lord
> Blessed is the man that feareth the lord
> That delighteth greatly in his commandments
> His seed shall be mighty upon earth
> The generation of the upright shall be blessed
> Wealth and riches shall be in his house
> And his righteousness endureth forever
> Psalm 112:1-3

> He will bless them that fears the Lord, both small and great
> The Lord shall increase you more and more, you and
> Your children, ye are blessed of the Lord
> Which made heaven and earth
> Psalm 115:13-15

> Blessed is every one that feareth the Lord
> That walketh in his ways, for thou shalt eat the labour
> of thine hands, happy shalt thou be, and it shall be well
> With thee
> Thy wife shall be as a fruitful vine by the sides of thine house
> Thy children like olive plants round about thy table
> Behold, that thus shall the man be blessed
> That feareth the lord
> Psalm 128:1-4

Perhaps it is not the blessings that should matter. It is the positioning of ourselves in relations with the Father, especially in terms of the reverential fear we have towards him in doing what we do that matters. If we love the Father with all our hearts, soul, mind and body to keep and do his will and commandments; we will also pursue the desires of his heart and mind, one of which is a heart that serves him with fear. It is one of the beautiful scriptures I find about the Father revealing a little bit of his heart's desire when it comes to fearing him. God said to Moses concerning the Israelites:

> O that there were such an heart in them
> That they would fear me and keep all my commandments always
> That it might be well with them and with their children forever!
> Deuteronomy 5:29

In the prophets' book of Malachi, God spoke through the prophet to draw the attention of his heart's desire for them to fear him. This was the period when their fear for the Lord was dwindled. Almost everyone did what they liked towards the things of God in terms of sacrifices, offerings and tithing. So God spoke to them through the prophet and said;

> A son honoureth the father and a servant his master
> If then I be a father where is my honour
> And if I be a master where is my fear
> Saith the Lord of hosts unto you
> O priests that despise my name
> And ye say, wherein have we despised thy name
> Malachi 1:6

Here, God directly asks us as his people, "where is my fear" to indicate his heart's desire for his people to fear him as their God whose word is final concerning them (Matthew 4:4). You see, when we do not do the things of God according to his will, according to his plan and according to his purpose; it is a sign of despising him. It is a sign of despising his name. And many people could be worshipping the Lord but not with their heart; despising him. As we have learnt, only things that are done with the heart and in the will of God please the Father and bring glory to him. Jesus also draws our attention to the fear of God in this wise when he said to the disciples;

> Why call me Lord, Lord
> And not do what I tell you?
> Luke 6:46
> (Matthew 7:24)

And then again our Lord Jesus Christ reveals to us that;

> Not everyone that saith to me Lord, Lord, shall enter into
> The kingdom of heaven, but he that doeth the will of
> My Father which is in heaven
> Matthew 7:21

Living by the will of God the Father, and living unto the will of God the Father is a sign of fearing him; and living by the fear of God the Father is in itself a treasure in the Believer. It is also a treasure unto the Lord;

> The Lord is exalted, for he dwelleth on high
> He has filled Zion with judgment and righteousness
> And wisdom and knowledge shall be the
> Stability of thy times, and strength of salvation
> The fear of the Lord is his treasure
> Isaiah 33:5-6

AS UNTO THE LORD

Laying up treasures in heaven involves a person's life in its entirety in connection with one's attitude in the use of what he or she has as talents, gifts and possessions of both material and spiritual things. It begins by learning how to use these things to bring glory to our God. This comes by simply doing things as unto God and not as unto man. The bible says this is because our reward comes from God and not from man. In other words, we should not look up to man in turn for our reward as we do anything with these gifts, talents and possessions to serve or minister unto mankind. We should not forget ourselves to be ministers of God, whoever you are in Christ, and that our duty is to God more than it is to man though it also concerns man. In other words, it is unto God and Christ that we have to look up to when we minister his word. So as the bible encourages us;

> And whatsoever ye do, do it heartily as to the Lord
> And not unto man, knowing that of the Lord ye shall
> Receive the reward of the inheritance
> For ye serve the Lord Christ
> Colossians 3:24

And again in the book of Ephesians, the bible says of us in Christ;

> For we are his workmanship created in Christ Jesus
> unto good works which God hath before ordained

> That we should walk in them
> Ephesians 2:10

These good works of God unto which we are ordained are done only in the name of our Lord, and also to his glory; whereby our heavenly account is credited with blessings. Hence the bible says to us:

> And whatsoever ye do in word or deed
> Do all in the name of the Lord Jesus
> Giving thanks to God and the Father
> By him
> Colossians 3:17

> Whether therefore ye eat or drink
> Whatsoever ye do, do all to the glory of God
> 1 Corinthians 10:31

Doing all things as unto the Lord can also mean doing it based upon the word and promises of God. It means doing it according to the plans of God. It means doing it according to the will of God. It means doing it by his faith. It means doing it by the love of God. It means doing it in the strength and the power he has given you.

FAITHFULNESS

Laying up treasures in heaven involves faithfulness or living by faith in its fullness towards the things of God. Faithfulness is one of the key factors in laying up treasures for ourselves in heaven. In other words, the more we believe the more and much fruit we bear. Believe is the key to not only bearing fruit but to also bring and see the manifestation of the fruit we bear. Hence, the just shall live by faith. Faith without works is dead and believe is faith at work; it is faith in action. The bible says that, God has counted us faithful to put us into his ministry (1 Timothy 1:12; Hosea 2:20); and that make us his faithful ministers. In this case, we should as well see ourselves as his word says, and count ourselves worthy of it to be faithful. Faithfulness in our thoughts, faithfulness in our utterances, faithfulness in our actions and faithfulness in our attitude and relations which has got much to do with how we handle the gifts, talents, possessions, callings and ministries of the Father in faith and in love based on the truth of his word. This is how the apostle Paul declared it;

> Let a man so account of us as of the ministers of Christ
> And stewards of the mysteries of God
> Moreover it is required in stewards that a man be found faithful
> 1 Corinthians 4:1-2
> (2 Corinthians 4:1-2)

As people of God, the bible says that, faithfulness is a requirement in handling the things or gifts, talents and possessions given unto us of God. We are only stewards but through faithfulness, they can yield rewards to our heavenly accounts. And then again, the apostle Paul speaking to Timothy concerning whom Timothy should commit the things of God said;

> And the things that thou hast heard of me
> Among many witnesses, the same commit
> Thou to faithful men who shall be able
> To teach others also
> 2 Timothy 2:2

Faithfulness includes the ability to impart or teach by the things, gifts, talents and possessions of God. In the book of revelations, the Lord in his letter to the church of Smyrna; encouraging them in their faithfulness in the face of tribulations said;

> Fear none of those things which thou shalt suffer:
> Behold, the devil shall cast some of you into prison,
> That ye may be tried; and ye shall have tribulation ten days

> Be thou faithful unto death and I will give thee
> A crown of life
> Revelation 2:10

Faithfulness enables us to be established, endure, persevere and overcome as winners, conquerors and as more than conquerors. It is actually the manifestation of God's own divine nature which is embodied in Christ who dwells in us; and which he has made us to be partakers of (2 Peter 1:4; Hebrews 12:10). God is himself faithful. This what the bible says about God being faithful;

> God is faithful by whom ye were called
> Unto the fellowship of his Son Jesus Christ our Lord
> 1 Corinthians 1:9
> (Deuteronomy 7:9)
> (1 Corinthians 10:13; 1 Thessalonians 5:24; 1 John 1:9; 1 Peter 4:19)

> Let us hold fast the profession of our faith
> Without wavering for he is faithful that promised
> Hebrews 10:23
> (Numbers 23:19; Titus 1:2; Hebrews 6:18; 2 Corinthians 1:20; 1 Peter 4; 19)

And the bible says that God's faithfulness is great (Lamentations 3:23), and that his faithfulness reaches out unto the clouds (Psalm 36:5; 1 John 1:9) and unto all generations (Psalm 119:90). However, it is not just the use of a talent, a gift or a possession that matters most, but it is actually the faithfulness attached in the use of these gifts, talents and possessions to bring glory to our Father that credits our heavenly account with rewards. Faithfulness then becomes an important factor of our lives in the kingdom of God and especially, when it comes to the laying up of treasures for ourselves in heaven (Matthew 6:19).

It is the faithful ones that are rewarded in the kingdom of heaven; and faithful ministers and servants are what the Father God seeks to make of us. God spoke through the prophet Hosea and said;

> And I will betroth thee unto me forever
> Yea, I will betroth thee unto me in righteousness, and in judgment,
> And in loving kindness, and in mercies
> I will even betroth thee unto me in faithfulness
> And thou shalt know the Lord
> Hosea 2:19-20

In faithfulness, we get to know God (John 17:3). In view of this prophecy, we should acknowledge how God had counted us faithful to position us in Christ as his ministers, servants and ambassadors. The apostle Paul who had a vision of how God has counted us faithful in Christ said;

> I thank Christ Jesus our Lord who hath enabled me
> For that he counted me faithful
> Putting me into the ministry
> 1Timothy 1:12

Faithfulness causes us to know God intimately and serve him faithfully with all our spirit, soul, mind and body. In other words, we are to be faithful in the way we think (Proverbs 23:7). We are to be faithful in our utterances (1Timothy 1:15; 2 Timothy 2:11; Titus 3:8; Titus 1:9; Romans 10:8). We are to be faithful in our deeds and actions (1 Thessalonians 1:3). We are to be faithful in all good works (Titus 2:14; Titus 3:1, 8; Ephesians 2:10); all in relations to God's gifts, callings and ministries for us; and also with one another to the praise and glory of our God and Father.

Concerning the parable of the talents, it is the faithful servant that got rewarded by his master; and being his servants, the Lord will rewards and blesses our faithfulness as well (1 Corinthians 4:1-2). We read of the faithful servant's reward;

> His lord said unto him
> Thou good and faithful servant thou hast been faithful
> Over a few things, I will make thee ruler over many things

Enter thou into the joy of thy lord
Matthew 25:21, 23
(Romans 5:17)

And the Lord said,

> Who then is that faithful and wise steward
> Whom his lord shall make ruler over his household to
> Give them their portion of meat in due time?
> Blessed is that servant whom his lord
> When he cometh shall find so doing
> Luke 12:42-43

And faithfulness does not have anything to do with the much or the less that a person may have or not have. It has to do more with the spirit and attitude of a person in connection with both what he has and what he does with it as he is supposed to bring glory, praise and thanksgiving to the Lord. This is what the bible says;

> He that is faithful in that which is least
> Is faithful also in much
> And he that is unjust in the least
> Is unjust also in much
> Luke 16:10

You can have little and be faithful with it, and you can have much and be faithful with it. Therefore, be it little or much, faithfulness is what counts. And so it is also in the kingdom of heaven that the faithful ones always will get rewarded and be blessed; all of which credits our heavenly account. The bible says;

> The faithful man shall abound with blessings
> But he that maketh haste to be rich
> Shall not be innocent
> Proverbs 28:20

And because it is the Father's will to reward and bless us, he has created, justified and counted us worthy of his kingdom (2Thessalonians 1:5) and also faithful to live by faith. Hence the just shall live by faith (Hebrews 10:38). Therefore, we should see and acknowledge living our lives by faith as:

His faithful ambassadors (2 Corinthians 5:20; Proverbs 13:17)

His faithful witnesses (Acts 1:8; Proverbs 14:5)

His faithful men and women (2 Timothy 2:2; Revelation 2:10; Proverbs 20:6; Luke 12:42-43)

His good and faithful servants (Matthew 25:21)

His wise and faithful stewards (Luke 12:42; 1 Corinthians 4:1-2)

His faithful ministers (1Timothy 1:12; 1 Corinthians 4:1-2; Ephesians 6:21)

For after all, it is his faithfulness that needs to be lived, declared and made known in and through our lives unto the world. And it is faithfulness that rewards, Amen.

FRUIT BEARING

Yet another way which contributes to the laying up of treasures for ourselves in heaven is fruit bearing or fruitfulness in the kingdom of heaven. Jesus said:

> Ye have not choosing me,
> But I have chosen you and ordained you,
> That you should go and bring forth fruit,
> And that your fruit should remain:
> That whatsoever ye shall ask of the Father

> In my name, he may give it you.
> John 15:16

Fruit bearing is essential in the kingdom of God to credit and account unto our heavenly account; and Our Lord Jesus Christ encourages us, not only to bear fruit but that the fruit which we bear should remain. In other words, the fruit we bear should be that which can remain and be accounted to our heavenly account. Right from the beginning of creation, God has pronounced the blessings of fruitfulness upon our lives to multiply, increase, abound and overflow to serve his purposes by taking dominion on this earth (Genesis 1:26-31). However, without being fruitful and multiplied, there cannot be any dominion; and without being able to replenish and subdue the earth, there cannot be any dominion. Dominion simply means reigning to rule with power and authority; in this case with us as the people of God in Christ who have been made kings and priests unto God (Revelation 5:10), we reign and rule by the power and the authority of God invested in us by his grace and righteousness. The bible which is God's word records this that;

> If by one man's offence death reigned by one
> Much more they which receive abundance
> Of grace and the gift of righteousness
> Shall reign in life by one, Jesus Christ
> Romans 5:17

Now, the amazing thing about fruitfulness or fruit bearing is the divine role it plays in ushering or translating and transferring us into that position of dominion. If we can catch and receive the revelation about fruitfulness and the role it plays in transferring us into that place and position of divine dominion, we would always desire and seek to maintain fruitfulness in every area of our lives as believers; spiritually, physically or materially, mentally and emotionally. In this way, we can learn to maintain our dominion to reign and rule in the power and authority of Christ in us (Luke 10:19).

We are blessed and purposed to be fruitful which leads to multiplication. Multiplication leads to increase. Increase leads to abundance. Abundance leads to the overflow for us to replenish and subdue. Overflow leads to dominion to reign and rule by serving and being a blessing unto others. See, we spiritually take dominion to reign and rule in and through Christ, as we serve and bless others with the good things of God in us (Matthew 23:11; Luke 9:48; Philemon 1:6). It is a form of giving, and it is a form of sowing that rewards our heavenly account.

There is the fruit of repentance (Matthew 3:8), and there is the fruit of righteousness (James 3:18; Hebrews 12:11; Philippians 1:11), all of which credits to our heavenly accounts as we bear them to God's glory. In fact there are many more fruits that we can bear, but what I would like to share is the importance of the desire and the zeal that we need to have to be fruitful. Therefore;

Seek to be fruitful in Christ (Genesis 1:28; Genesis 9:1, 7; Philippians 4:19).

Seek to be multiplied in Christ (Genesis 1:28; Genesis 9:1, 7; 1Peter 1:2; 2Peter 1:2; Jude 1:2; Genesis 17:2).

Seek to be increased in Christ (Luke 2:52; Deuteronomy 16:15; Psalm 62:10; Proverbs 1:5; Isaiah 29:19; Luke 17:5; 1 Corinthians 3:6; 2 Corinthians 9:10; Colossians 2:19).

Seek to abound in Christ (John 10:10; Philippians 4:12; Proverbs 28:20; 1Corinthians 15:58; Philippians 1:9; Colossians 2:6-7; 1Thessalonians 3:12; 2Peter 1:8).

Seek to be abundant and overflowing in Christ (Exodus 34:5; John 10:10; Matthew 13:12; Ephesians 3:20; 1Peter 1:3; Deuteronomy 28:47).

Seek to be a blessing in Christ (Genesis 12:2; Galatians 3:13-14; Ephesians 1:3; Psalm 3:8; Proverbs 10:6, 22; Proverbs 28:20; 1Timothy 1:12; James 3:10).

Seek to take dominion in Christ to reign and to rule by becoming fruitful with the good things of God which are in you because of Christ (Philemon 1:6). It is only by the good things of God that we can take dominion over situations and circumstances in life.

Bearing fruit to our heavenly account enables us also to receive from it, hence, whatsoever ye shall ask of the Father in my name, says Jesus, He may give it you. Another thing we need to consider in terms of fruit bearing or fruitfulness is that, the Lord has declared and chosen us for the main purpose of bearing fruit in the kingdom. It therefore means that, we as his chosen ones should live and walk in the awareness of a fruit bearing attitude. We should have a divine vision and purpose of bearing fruit. It becomes an important word to consider in our kingdom lifestyle. In this case, it becomes quite interesting then, to know the ways by which we can bear fruit in the kingdom to God's glory; some of which we talked about already.

It is interesting to know that, if a person does not have an account with a bank, he cannot put, lay nor keep his money or other things he treasures like gold and jewels into that bank. The person first has to open an account with that bank before they can give him a number or a code by which he can operate with that bank. Similarly, for the bible to tell us to lay up treasures in heaven implies that, there is an account there for us; and as we have talked about, this account which is a heavenly one came about because of Christ. The Lord encouraging us to be rich towards heaven and God, said to us;

> Lay not for yourselves treasures upon earth,
> Where moth and rust doth corrupt,
> And where thieves break in and steal,
> But lay up for yourselves; treasures in heaven

> Where neither moth nor rust doth corrupt,
> Where thieves do not break through, nor steal.
> Matthew 6:19-21

Now, laying up treasures, bearing of fruit and sowing; either to the flesh or the spirit involves our spirit, soul, mind and body. It also involves our thoughts, deeds, utterances and actions and how we use all these things combined to glorify the Father. These all contribute to the laying up treasures for ourselves in heaven depending on how we live by them on earth. The good news is that, the Father has given us of his Spirit who, as a creative, power and life giving Spirit (Romans 8:11); is also a fruit bearing Spirit (John 15:16; Isaiah 32:15-18; Galatians 5:22-25). And by him, in him, with him and through him, we are able to bear fruit unto the Father's glory by the grace of God.

EVANGELISM

However, one of the most important things to laying up treasures in heaven is through evangelism, or bringing the gospel of Jesus Christ to other people. Through evangelism, we give and sow with our time, talents and finance. Jesus said: "I have chosen you that you should go and bring forth fruit." To where do the Lord say we should go? Into all nations of the world and preach the gospel to every creature. (Mark 15:15).

It is not just the doing that bears fruit to our heavenly account. Neither is it just the doing of these things that brings glory to the Father; but the doing of it with all our hearts, in his name, according to his will, plans and purposes that bears fruit to our heavenly account.

Not only that; but everything that we do in the name of Christ; directly or indirectly to win and bring a soul into the kingdom of God accounts to our heavenly bank. No wonder the bible says that, the whole heavens rejoice at the repentance and saving of a soul. The revelation here is that, whatever and everything that one does to cause heaven to rejoice, adds to our heavenly account as far as evangelism and mission works are concerned.

The apostle Paul reveals in most of his letters to the churches about how they shared in his grace and blessings (Philippians 1:7); as well as his sufferings on the mission fields though they might not physically be there with him. But most of the times, they shared in all these things with him because of what they might have done; directly or indirectly to help and support his mission works, some of these things they might have done in cash or kind. Even through prayers. As we read his letters, we could see that there were many times the apostle Paul asked to be remembered in the prayers of the saints as he was on the mission field (Colossians 4:3-4; Ephesians 6:18-19). All these contributed to the apostle as a seed in his life bearing fruit unto the heavenly accounts of them that were involved directly and indirectly. It also contributed to the sharing of the apostle's grace and sufferings. It is what he referred to as love in the spirit (Colossians 1:8)

In reference to a similar instance concerning the Philippians church, the apostle Paul, who was aware of the fruits born out of such support made it clear to the Philippians church and said;

> Not because I desire a gift
> But I desire fruit that may abound
> To your account
> Philippians 4:17

There is always a reward for evangelizing the gospel of Christ. The Lord Jesus Christ spoke of how the whole of heaven rejoices at the saving of one soul. And every time we do something to bring joy unto heaven, it credits our heavenly account. The apostle Paul said;

> For though I preach the gospel, I have nothing to glory of:
> For necessity is laid upon me yea, woe is unto me
> If I preach not the gospel, for if I do this thing willingly

> I have a reward but if against my will, a dispensation of
> The gospel is committed unto me, what is my reward then?
> Verily that when I preach the gospel I may make the gospel of Christ
> Without charge that I abuse not my power in the gospel
> 1 Corinthians 9:16-18

There is therefore a reward in preaching the gospel of Christ to win souls. After all, it is for the more reason why our Lord Jesus Christ came down from heaven to earth. The bible says;

> For God sent not his Son into the world
> To condemn the world but that the world
> Through him might be saved
> John 3:17

> For the Son of man is come to save
> That which was lost
> Matthew 18:11

> For the Son of man is not come to
> Destroy men's lives but to save them...
> Luke 9:56

And the price of the saved souls of men is the life, death, burial and resurrection of Christ; where he suffered to shed his blood for the sinful nature of men. It is the more reason why the apostle Peter said that we are not redeemed with corruptible things through tradition but with the precious blood of Christ; as of a lamb without blemish and without spot (1 Peter 1:18- 19)

The blood of Christ for the salvation of man's soul is already shed and has redeemed all men; so that all men everywhere can call upon him to be saved (Romans 10:13) and come to the knowledge of the truth (1 Timothy 2:3-5) which can make them free (John 8:36). We should therefore go forth by his great commission for us, to win souls into the kingdom of God.

And Jesus came and spake unto them
Saying, all power is giving unto me in heaven and in earth
Go ye therefore, and teach all nations baptizing them in the name of
The Father, and of the Son, and of the Holy Ghost teaching them
to observe all things whatsoever I have commanded you
And lo, I am with you always even unto the end of
The world Amen
Matthew 28:18-20

And he said unto them go ye into all the world
And preach the gospel to every creature
Mark 16:15

GIVING

Another area whereby we can lay up treasures for ourselves in heaven is giving based on kingdom biblical principles of faith and love. Why faith and love? Because those are the two closest connected to the heart, and our giving must be done with the heart and from the heart. God is interested only in the things which we do with and from the heart, giving included; and the purpose of it all is to glorify our God and our Father who is in heaven. While we glorify God with the things we do with and from our hearts, he blesses us by crediting our heavenly accounts.

And whatsoever ye do in word or deed,
Do all in the name of the Lord Jesus,
Giving thanks to God and the Father by him...
And whatsoever ye do, do it heartily,
As to the Lord, and not unto man
Knowing that of the Lord ye shall receive
The reward of the inheritance
For ye serve the Lord Christ.
Colossians 3:17, 23-24
(Genesis 15:1; Heb. 11:6)

It is only when we do things from our heart, especially in connection with the kingdom principles that we get blessed and the Father is glorified.

> Whether therefore ye eat, or drink,
> Or whatsoever ye do,
> Do all to the glory of God.
> 1 Corinthians 10:31

It is important to learn how to do everything with the heart and from the heart, as far as the principles of the kingdom is concerned, and especially if we want to glorify God and be blessed in our lives.

The very first time God asked the Israelites to give to build a sanctuary unto him, it was their heart he looked to receive from them. God was not even concerned with what they were to bring but the willingness of their heart to do it. The joy and the desire with which they were to do it was what I believe God was looking for. It was not the quantity or even the quality. Amazingly, God was not even concerned with what he asked them to bring. It was their heart. I may not know and perhaps not be able to understand it fully, but what was revealed to me is that, God, the Father seeks to be glorified and that only through what is done with the heart is that which glorifies him. He said to Moses:

> And the Lord spake unto Moses, saying,
> Speak unto the children of Israel, that they bring me an offering:
> Of every man that giveth it willingly with his heart,
> Ye shall take my offering...
> And let them make me a sanctuary,
> That I may dwell among them
> Exodus 25:1, 2, 8

If it is for the Lord, it should bring glory to him. If it is unto the Lord it should bless us and if is for the Lord, it should be done willingly, joyfully and gladly with all our heart; in faith and in love. These are some of the principles by which our heavenly account gets credited by the Lord.

> And Moses spake unto all the congregation of
> The children of Israel, saying,
> This is the thing which the Lord commanded saying,
> Take ye from among you an offering unto the Lord,
> Whosoever is of a willing heart
> Let him bring it, an offering of the Lord…
> Exodus 35:4-5

Many times, we may get tempted to do things for the Lord, but with an attitude which is not of the Holy Spirit: without faith, without love, without joy and without gladness; no passion and affection from our heart for the Lord, in whose name we are supposed to do everything (Colossians 3:17, 23).

It is time that the children of the kingdom of God realized that, when the bible spoke of not being conformed to this world, it partly includes the attitude by which we do things as well unto the Lord and his name; which includes given. We do not have to follow the world systems to do what we do. There might be national, societal, traditional, tribal and even familial ways of attitudes in doing things; but when it comes to the things of God, it takes a total different turn. Here, it is the heart that matters; coupled with the motives and attitudes which take the divine principles of God and his kingdom to do it. It might be easier to get accustomed to the rituals of the things of God without any attachment of the heart. Our Lord Jesus Christ spoke a scripture which helps throw some light on it. He said concerning people whose hearts are not in what they did unto the Lord;

> And in them is fulfilled the prophecy of Esaias
> Which saith, by hearing ye shall hear and shall not understand
> And seeing ye shall see and shall not perceive
> For this people's heart is waxed gross and their ears are dull
> Of hearing and their eyes they have closed

> Lest at any time they should see with their eyes
> And hear with their ears and should understand with their heart
> And should be converted and I should heal them
> Matthew 13:14-15

These are not automatic principles, but that which have to be learned and applied by the power of the Holy Spirit of God who dwells in us. Without applying the revelation knowledge of God's word, there will be no manifestation of the spirit, life, power and the anointing of the word in the situation and the purpose for which they are meant.

In his address to the church in Corinth concerning giving and receiving, Paul encouraged them to give with their heart in order to receive back and be blessed of the Lord. He said;

> Every man according as he purposes in his heart,
> So let him give; not grudgingly, or of necessity;
> For God loveth a cheerful giver.
> 2 Corinthians 9:7-8

A cheerful giver is the person who gives willingly joyful out of the heart in assurance of faith that God would cause men to give back in returns; good measure, pressed down, and shaken together and running over. He is the person that gives out of a willing joyful heart without expecting back from human sources, knowing that the Lord will give exceedingly abundantly in returns out of his open heavens to pour out and release his blessings. Jesus said and taught us this way;

> But love ye your enemies
> And do good and lend, hoping for nothing
> Again; and your reward shall be great
> And ye shall be the children of the highest
> For he is kind unto the unthankful
> And to the evil
> Luke 6:35

Then again the apostle Paul went on to state clearly however that, depending on how much one gives, the same shall be given in return to that person or credited back unto him. He said;

> But this I say,
> He which soweth sparingly shall reap also sparingly
> And he which soweth bountifully
> Shall reap also bountifully
> 2 Corinthians 9:6

It is the blessing in giving and the glory it gives, or brings to the Father that should motivate us to give, rather, not the thing that is being giving. Quite often, it is not the object being given that matters to the Father; but the motivational spirit by which we do what we do in his name and unto him (Exodus 25:1-2). This is also how our heavenly account gets credited or rewarded by the Lord. The apostle Paul reminded us in the book of Acts to remember the word of the Lord Jesus Christ which says that it is more blessing to give than to receive (Acts 20:35). This is what he said;

> Give and it shall be given unto you
> Good measure, pressed down, and shaken together,
> And running over shall men give into your bosom
> For with the same measure that
> Ye mete withal, it shall be measured to you again
> Luke 6:38

We give to lay up treasures for ourselves in heaven through our offerings unto the Lord.

We give to lay up treasures for ourselves in heaven through sowing.

We give to lay up treasures for ourselves in heaven through tithing.

We give to lay up treasures for ourselves in heaven through alms to the poor or the needy.

GIVING TO THE POOR

The poor simply means someone who is in need or the needy. One who when you give cannot give or pay back as you expect. It is God that rewards us when we give this way to the poor. I believe these are the kinds that the Lord had in mind when he taught us concerning giving without expecting back.

> And if ye do good to them which do good to you
> What thank have ye?
> For sinners also do even the same
> And if ye lend to them of whom
> Ye hope to receive, what thank have ye
> For sinners also lend to sinners
> To receive as much again
> Luke 6:33-34

Giving to the poor or the needy should always be understood from God's perspective. It is the only means of giving where the bible reveals as lending unto the Lord. Now if we lend to the Lord and the Lord is going to pay us back, we can just imagine how much it is going to be; both in quality and quantity. This is what the word of God says about given to the poor;

> He that hath pity upon the poor,
> Lendeth unto the Lord
> And that which he has given will he pay him again.
> Proverbs 19:17
> (Psalm 112:5; Psalm 37:26)

It is even an honour unto the Lord to give to the poor and needy in the name of the Lord. In other words, one of the practical ways of honoring the Lord with our giving is to give to the poor. The bible says;

> He that oppresseth the poor reproacheth his maker
> But he that honoureth him

Hath mercy on the poor
Proverbs 14:31

GOOD WORKS

We should not misunderstand to misinterpret God's principle of giving and receiving and limit it to only money; and for that matter, material things. It goes beyond that, though it plays part. Many people may not realize but giving involves the spirit, soul, mind and body. It involves our entire being. However, it is primarily done with the heart as the focal point of activity and motivation. We give materially, in cash and kind; but we also give spiritually through faith, love, joy and peace; even in and through prayer. Jesus said, "Freely you have received, and freely you have to give." (Matthew 1:8)

Now, how have we received freely? And what have we received freely? It is very important to know, especially if you are a citizen of the Royal Kingdom of God. If you know what you have received and how you received it, then you will know what you have and can learn how to give freely. A man can only give what he has. Many people in the royal kingdom of God do not know what they have freely received and therefore do not know what they have. So they cannot enjoy from it. Since they can't enjoy from it, it becomes difficult for them to give willingly out of what they have received of the Lord from the heart. These are some of the means through which the enemy takes advantage to steal one's blessings in Christ by keeping us from giving. It shows how important it should mean for us to do all things with and out of our heart; especially when it has to do with given in the name of the Lord. As Believers and royals of God's kingdom, we should also know the kind of heart that is in us, just as we should know the spirit that is in us (John 9:55; Ezekiel 36:26, 27). As believers in Christ, the heart which you receive as a born again person, makes you a cheerful giver and it also gives you the ability to give freely. And to give freely means giving by faith with love, joy and gladness from a willing heart. This is something which comes only by the power of God's Holy Spirit that dwells in you.

We receive freely of God and from God through Christ, in whom the bible says, dwell all the fullness and everything that pertains to life and godliness. Now the bible says that we are joint-heirs with Christ, and therefore we share everything also with him. These include his divine abilities, one of which giving with a willing heart is one.

And the bible says that when we have given willingly and joyfully from out of our heart, God is also able to make and cause all grace to abound toward us in order for us to always have all sufficiency in all things (that pertains to life and godliness here on earth... 2 Peter 1:3), that we may abound (and overflow) unto every good work and be a blessing unto others. (Emphasis is personal). This is what the bible says;

> And God is able to make all grace
> Abound toward you
> That ye always having all sufficiency
> In all things may abound to every
> Good work
> 2 Corinthians 9:8

> For we are the workmanship of God
> Created in Christ Jesus unto good works
> Which God hath before ordained
> That we should walk in them (unto his glory)
> Ephesians 1:10

And the good works of the Lord are done with a willing and joyful heart. If we can consider giving as some of the good works, then it becomes necessarily important to know why it should be done from the heart.

> ...For the Lord seeth not as man seeth;
> For man looketh on the outward appearance,

> But the Lord looketh on the heart.
> 1 Samuel 16:7

The apostle Paul in his epistles to the churches use to encourage the believers concerning the good works which God before ordained that we should walk in them. Not only for them, but I also believe that, those words of edification were meant for us as well. The good works are also meant for us to walk in them; in other words, it should become part of our daily godly life. He said to the believers in Thessalonica:

> But ye, brethren, be not weary in well doing
> 2 Thessalonians 3:13

He encouraged the believers in Galatia:

> And let us not be weary in well doing:
> For in due season we shall reap, if we faint not
> As we have therefore opportunity, let us do good
> Especially unto them who are of the household of faith.
> Galatians 6:9-10

Well doing and good works are the same. In Titus chapter 3, Paul not only encourages us to be ready unto every good work, (v.1). In other words, to be readily and willingly out of a joyful heart to do the good works; and he also admonishes us as believers, to learn and maintain good works, which is necessary to make us fruitful unto our heavenly account. He said in speaking to Titus;

> This is a faithful saying,
> And these things I will that thou affirm constantly,
> That they which have believed in God might be careful
> to maintain good works, these things are good
> And profitable unto men
> Titus 3:8

Learning to maintain good works mean that, we are not to get weary and not to get fainted or discouraged in the course of our doing these good works of the Lord (Luke 6:35-36). This comes by the power of the Holy Spirit. It means that, we should not allow any man or any situation to become an offence, a stumbling block or an excuse for us to stop our good works. After all, it is not man, but God who has ordained for us to walk in them to bring glory unto him. That is how we get blessed from doing them (1 Corinthians 10:31; Colossians 3:17; Colossians 3:23-24).

It is good also to know that all our inheritance in Christ, all the promises of God for us in Christ, all the blessings of God for us in Christ and all the fruits which we bear in Christ by whom and through whom God the Father supplies to meet every need of his children (Philippians 4:19); all combine together and contribute to the resources out of which we lay up treasures for ourselves in heaven.

Through giving willingly and from the heart, we not only layup treasures, we also bear fruit to our heavenly account. Paul, in reference to the encouragement that our Lord Jesus Christ gave us concerning giving and receiving, before ascending to heaven; and now seated in the Father's right hand said in Acts 20:35 to remember the words of the Lord Jesus, how he said, "It is more blessed to give than to receive."

> Give and it shall be given unto you
> Good measure, pressed down, and shaken together,
> And running over, shall men give into your bosom (account)
> For with the same measure that ye mete withal
> It shall be measured to you again.
> Luke 6:38

SOWING AND REAPING

Whatever a sows, that shall account to his heavenly treasures and whatever a man sows, that shall he also reap out of his heavenly account. Perhaps also, in the place where a man sows, it is there also that he can reap from. There is the need for a seed and there is the need for a place or a ground to sow into as far as the principle of sowing and reaping is concerned (Luke 8:4-15). However, it God who gives the seed by his word and promises (Isaiah 55:10- 11; 2 Corinthians 9:10-11; Luke 8:11; Luke 6:43-45). It is also him that watches over its germination to grow and multiplies to increase the fruit thereof (2 Corinthians 3:6-9; 9:10-11). What we need to do is just sow the seed which he gives. As we sow the seed God gives us out of our heart and according to his will on a good ground or place, he will do the rest for us to be blessed by the fruit of the seed we have sown. Now, everything that God has given unto us in Christ serves as a seed from God's perspective and therefore can be sown to bear fruit. And knowing what God has given to us in life as seed also enables us also to sow and reap. It is good to know that everything in connection to our life in Christ right here on earth, directly and indirectly serves as a seed that can be released and sown as a seed. And everything that God has given us in connection with our heavenly account can also be released and sown as a seed. A seed has to be treasured if we expect to reap a good harvest. This means that it should not be sown just anyhow, and it should not be sown just anywhere to expect a right harvest.

The Father expects us to sow the seed he gives us, but he also expects us to sow it on a good ground in order for it to be fruitful in returns. In the same way we who sow should do so in faith, while expecting to reap in returns; just like a farmer who plows and sows a seed. He also expects to reap a harvest in returns.

Of course, money is also a seed but it is not the only thing that serves a seed in life. And you can sow money and reap money according to the divine principle of sowing and reaping. And since everything we sow credits our heavenly account, money sown as seed and credited with our heavenly account gives us right to claim money from heaven in times of financial needs (Hebrews 4:16). Everything in life becomes seed when it is released towards the kingdom of heaven to lay up treasures for ourselves in heaven. In this case love, joy, peace, attitudes of righteousness and holiness all become seeds that can be sown. Also obedience, hearing and acting upon the word of God in faith are all forms of seed and a way of sowing a seed when they are applied to our lives in faith.

As we sow into the kingdom of God, we are laying up treasures for ourselves in heaven. However, we can only reap what we sow but cannot reap what we have not sown. We can only give what we have. We cannot give what we don't have. Just like the other ways of laying up treasures for ourselves in heaven; sowing is done from the heart, in faith with love and joy. We sow material things. We also sow spiritual things. But just as the divine principle of sowing and reaping goes; one reaps what he sows. The bible says;

Be not deceived; God is not mocked

> For whatsoever a man soweth that shall he also reap
> For he that soweth to the flesh shall of the flesh reap corruption
> But he that soweth to the Spirit shall of the Spirit reap
> Life everlasting
> Galatians 6:7-8

Sowing for increase corresponds also with the quality and quantity of the seed sown, as the apostle Paul reveals;

> But this I say
> He which soweth sparingly shall reap
> Also sparingly, and he which soweth
> Bountifully shall reap also bountifully
> 2 Corinthians 9:6

> He that has a bountiful eye shall be blessed
> For he giveth of his bread to the poor
> Proverbs 22:9

The bible says that we sow in tears but reap in joy (Psalm 126:5); perhaps meaning that, the periods of sowing might not be all that pleasant. There are works involve; plowing of the land, preparing the grounds to sow and the sowing itself to the times of waiting to have a taste of the fruit all go together for sowing to be in tears. But when the fruit is there and we begin to reap and harvest; it turns out to become a moment of joy. It is good to know that the whole purpose of sowing is actually to lay up treasures for ourselves in heaven, but like all the many things that the bible reveals concerning the laying up of treasures for ourselves; it is also to show the position of our hearts. This is because it takes doing with the heart to credit our heavenly account. Hence the bible says, where your treasure is, there also will your heart be. The point of the truth is that, whatever is not sown with the heart shall not bear any fruit to our heavenly account or treasures. And who would want to sow and not reap anyway? A corrupt heart and a deceitful heart will in no way yield anything successful in the kingdom of God (Micah 6:12-15). This is how the bible in the King James Version puts it;

> The wicked worketh a deceitful work
> But to him that soweth righteousness
> Shall be a sure reward
> Proverbs 11:18
> (James 3:18)

> He that soweth iniquity shall reap vanity
> And the rod of his anger shall fail
> Proverbs 22:8

> Even as I have seen
> They that plow iniquity and sow wickedness reap the same
> Job 4:8

CHAPTER FIVE

ACCESSING THE HEAVENLY ACCOUNTS

◇◇◇◇◇◇◇◇◇◇◇◇◇◇◇◇◇◇◇◇◇◇

Knowing that you have a heavenly account and knowing that you have treasures laid up for you in this account also gives you a right and the authority to access and enjoy the fruit of these treasures. There are times when we have sown and waited for the harvest of the fruit, and there are times when we need to partake and enjoy of that which we have harvested and reaped. Like the word of God says;

> To everything there is a season
> And a time to every purpose under the heaven
> A time to be born and a time to die
> A time to plant and a time to pluck up
> That which is planted
> Ecclesiastes 3:1-2

However in terms of our heavenly account which has to do with the tapping in of all the spiritual blessings, the promises and the divine inheritance of God for us in Christ; we need to know and learn how to position ourselves well in order to receive, live and walk in them according to the Father's will unto his glory. And though we may not be able to put all and everything down in this little book; we would however take a look at some of the ways by which we can position ourselves, the first of which I believe is the incorruptible seed of God's word. It is the foundation of laying up treasures in heaven; and it is the foundation for accessing our treasures in the heavenly places, the bible says;

> Blessed is the man that walketh not in the counsel
> Of the ungodly nor standeth in the way of sinners
> Nor sitteth in the seat of the scornful
> But his delight is in the law of the Lord
> And in his law doth he meditate day and night
> And he shall be like a tree planteth by the rivers of water
> That bringeth forth his fruit in his season
> His leaf also shall not wither
> And whatsoever he doeth shall prosper
> Psalm 1:1-3
> (Joshua 1:8)

Our heavenly account is purposed for us to prosper in the kingdom of heaven right here on earth, and not after. And the word, laws and commandments of God are what we need and have on this earth to guide us into the inheritance, promises, blessings, favour and prosperity of God for us in Christ by which we need to live. Again, it is by the word of God that we are able to know what are truly ours in God (1 Corinthians 2:9), as we live a godly life on this earth. The apostle Paul said in his farewell speech to the elders of the church in Ephesus;

> And now brethren I commend you to God and
> to the word of his grace which is able to build you up
> And to give you an inheritance among
> All them which are sanctified
> Acts 20:32

Then again, the Lord spoke and said unto Joshua directing him in how Joshua could make his ways prosperous in the Lords presence which was only by the word, laws and commandments of the Lord. The Lord said unto Joshua;

> This book of the law shall not depart
> Out of thy mouth but thou shalt meditate therein
> Day and night that thou mayest observe to do
> According to all that is written therein
> For then thou shalt make thy way prosperous
> And have a good success
> Joshua 1:8

The apostle John also points to add something important to the fulfillment of our prosperity when he said;

> Beloved, I wish above all things
> That thou mayest prosper and be in health
> Even as thy soul prospereth
> 3 John 1:2

And it takes the word of God to cause our soul to prosper in health (Proverbs 4:20-22). So we realize how our prosperity and good success in connection to our heavenly account is tied to the word of God. It therefore becomes important in our lives; the role the word of God plays to bring to pass the manifestation of all that fulfills our heavenly account. It also becomes important concerning our attitude towards the hearing, receiving, believing and acting upon the word of God, so that we can be well positioned to access our heavenly account. Let us take a look to some few.

HEARING THE VOICE OF THE LORD

> If thou will diligently hearken to the voice of the Lord thy God
> And wilt do that which is right in his sight
> And wilt give ear to his commandments
> And keep all his statutes
> I will put none of these diseases upon thee
> Which I have brought upon the Egyptians
> For I am the Lord that healeth thee

Exodus 15:26
(Deuteronomy 7:12, 15)

And it shall come to pass
If thou shalt hearken diligently unto the voice of the Lord thy God
To observe and to do all his commandments
Which I command thee this day that the Lord thy God will set thee
Above all nations of the earth and all these blessings
shall come on thee
And overtake thee, if thou shalt hearken
Unto the voice of the Lord thy God
Deuteronomy 28:1-2

OBEYING THE VOICE OF THE LORD

If ye be willing and obedient
Ye shall eat the good of the land
But if ye refuse and rebel
Ye shall be devoured with the sword
For the mouth of the LORD hath spoken it
Isaiah 1:19-20

And Samuel said,
Hath the Lord as great delight in burnt offerings and sacrifices
As in obeying the voice of the Lord?
Behold to obey is better than sacrifice
And to hearken than the fat of rams
1 Samuel 15:22

BELIEVING THE WORD OF THE LORD

Jesus saith unto him
Thomas because thou hast seen me
Thou hast believed

Blessed are they that have not seen
And yet have believed
John 20:29

And blessed is she that believed
For there shall be a performance
Of those things which were told
Her of the Lord
Luke 1:45

I had fainted, unless I had believed
To see the goodness of the Lord
In the land of the living
Psalm 27:13

HONOURING THE LORD

Honour the Lord with thy substance
And with the first fruits of all thy increase
So shall thy barns be filled with plenty
And thy presses shall burst out
With new wine
Proverbs 3:9-10

ACTING UPON THE WORD OF THE LORD

But be ye doers of the word
And not hearers only
Deceiving your own selves
James 1:22

But he said
Yea rather, blessed are they that hear the word of God
And keep it

Alfred Prempeh-Dapaah

Luke 11:28
(John 14:15, 21, 23)

And Simon answering said unto him
Master we have toiled all the night and have taken nothing
Nevertheless at thy word I will let down the net
Luke 5:5
(Luke 1:38)

TITHING UNTO THE LORD

Bring ye all the tithes into the storehouse
That there may be meat in my house
And prove me now herewith
Saith the Lord of host
If I will not open you the windows
Of heaven and pour you out a blessing
That there shall not be room enough
To receive it
Malachi 3:10

OFFERING UNTO THE LORD

We offer unto the Lord through thanksgiving, praise and worship. And offering can be in the form of material kind or cash. The Psalmist said;

Offer unto God thanksgiving
And pay thy vows unto the most high
And call upon me in the day of trouble
I will deliver thee and thou shalt
Glorify me
Psalm 50:14-15

> Whoso offereth praise glorifieth me
> And to him that ordereth his conversation
> Aright will I show the salvation of God
> Psalm 50:23
> (James 3:2)

> By him therefore
> Let us offer the sacrifice of praise to God
> Continually, that is the fruit of our lips
> Giving thanks in his name
> Hebrews 13:15

They might not be much, and these are not all; but the above are some of the ways by which we can meditate to position ourselves to access and enjoy the abundance and the overflow of our heavenly accounts. However, just positioning ourselves for them is not enough; we need to get them to be manifested, demonstrated and experienced in our personal lives right here on earth. That is where prayer and fasting, living by faith and walking in love become very important in our lives as believers. By faith we pray ourselves into agreement with God the Father concerning all his blessings, promises and inheritance for us in Christ. Praying ourselves into agreement with the Father is how we make it possible for ourselves to believe for them (Amos 3:3; Matthew 19:26; Mark 9:23). By faith we access our heavenly account of God's abundant grace and glory for us in Christ (1 Peter 5:10; 2 Peter 1:3; Romans 5:1-2). By faith we receive from our heavenly account all the blessings of the Father for us in Christ (Galatians 3:14). By faith we usher ourselves into the manifestation of all that we receive as promises and blessings out of our heavenly accounts (Ephesians 1:3; 2 Peter 1:4). Hence, the Just shall live by faith (Romans 1:17); and in living by faith, we believe until we have seen the results of what we are believing God for (Hebrews 10:38-39; Psalm 27:13).

CHAPTER SIX

LIVING UNDER OPEN HEAVENS

◇◇◇◇◇◇◇◇◇◇◇◇◇◇◇◇◇◇◇◇

Give willingly from the heart, as unto the Lord, by faith, in love, with joy and gladness; and you will see how God will also cause all grace to abound unto you. This grace would cause you to increase, abound and overflow in blessing, favor and prosperity. He will use this abundance of grace to divinely cause men to give to you, pressed down; shaken and running over that you will in turn be a blessing unto others and the kingdom. Thus we end up in what I term as God's total provision and continuous supply where there is no poverty, lack or leanness, but all plenty, abundance and overflow…

Once again, God does not force one to give. He does not manipulate man to give. Not even the how much you have or not have. The word is GIVE but in giving to him, it is the heart that God pays attention to. Therefore, let giving be with your heart, and from your heart. This includes everything that makes one be able to give willingly from the heart with faith, love, joy and gladness. Whatever God asks a person to do, it is by the heart that he measures to accept or reject one's work. This can be seen in the case of Cain and Abel. The story can be read in Genesis chapter 4.

There are many things we can learn about God and his faithfulness, when says we should do something.

Alfred Prempeh-Dapaah

GOD'S FAITHFULNESS

God, the Father will not tell us to do anything which he knows is beyond our capacity or something which he has not equipped us for through his word or his Spirit that dwells in us. He is a just and a faithful God. He will not tell us to do anything which he knows he has not equipped us for. The bible says that his faithfulness is great (Lamentations 3:23) and that, it reaches out even unto the clouds (Psalm 36:5). It means that, God does everything by his word as he has promised in his Son Jesus Christ to bless, favor and prosper us; all of which is based upon his faithfulness. It is therefore important to know some areas of his faithfulness to understand his blessings, favor and prosperity towards us. He is faithful with himself as God. He is faithful with his word and promises. He is faithful with his works. He is faithful with his creation, and that includes you. In talking about the Lord's faithfulness, this is what the bible says;

> Know therefore that the Lord thy God,
> He is God, the faithful God,
> Which keepeth covenant and mercy with them
> That love him and keep his commandments
> To a thousand generations.
> Deuteronomy 7:9

God the Father is faithful to keep covenant and mercy with us that love him and keep his commandments. And by keeping covenant and mercy with us that love him, he causes all things to work out good for our good. This is also because, by loving and keeping his commandments; we are brought into the purpose of his calling (John 14:15, 21, 23; Romans 8:28)

> Thus saith the Lord, the Redeemer of Israel and his Holy One,
> to him whom man despiseth, to him whom the nation abhorreth,
> To a servant of rulers, Kings shall see and arise,
> Princes also shall worship, because of the Lord that is faithful,

Laying Up Treasures In Heaven

And the Holy One of Israel and he shall choose thee.
Isaiah 49: 7

God is faithful, by whom ye are called
Unto the fellowship of his Son Jesus Christ
Our Lord
1 Corinthians 1:9

Faithful is he that called you, who also will do it
1 Thessalonians 5:24

Let us hold fast the profession of our faith
Without wavering; for he is faithful that promised.
Hebrews 10:23
(Hebrews 11:11; 1 Peter 5:19)

In his Faithfulness, he forgives us our sins, and delivers us from temptations.

If we confess our sins, he is faithful and just
to forgive us our sins,
And to cleanse us from all unrighteousness
1 John 1:9
(Psalm 103:3)

There hath no temptation taken you
But such as is common to man;
But God is faithful, who will not suffer you
To be tempted above that ye are able;
But will with the temptation also make a way
To escape, that ye may be able to bear it
1 Corinthians 10:13

In his faithfulness, he establishes us in his will, plans and purposes.

> But the Lord is faithful, who shall establish you,
> And keep you from evil.
> 2 Thessalonians 3:3

> But the God of all grace, who has called us unto
> His eternal glory by Christ Jesus,
> After that ye have suffered a while,
> Make you perfect, stablish, strengthen, settle you.
> To him be glory and dominion, forever and ever. Amen
> 1 Peter 5:10, 11

> Now he which stablisheth us with you in Christ
> And hath anointed us is God
> Who hath also sealed us, and given the earnest of
> The Spirit in our hearts.
> 2 Corinthians 1:21-22

In his faithfulness, God counts us worthy and calls, appoints, anoints and establishes us as his royal ministers, ambassadors, servants, vessels of honour, workmanship and co-workers in his kingdom. The apostle Paul in his letter to his spiritual son, Timothy, puts it this way.

> I thank Christ Jesus our Lord, who hath enabled me,
> For he counted me faithful, putting me into the ministry;
> 1Timothy 1:12

In his faithfulness, God keeps his word and brings to pass, whatever he promises unto a good and a successful end. The apostle Paul again, who knew and understood the faithfulness of God said concerning the Philippians' church;

> I thank my God upon every remembrance of you,
> Always in every prayer of mine for you all
> Making request with joy, for your fellowship in
> The gospel from the first day until now,
> Being confident of this very thing, that he which has

> Begun a good work in you will perform it
> Until the day of Jesus Christ
> Philippians 1:6

In his faithfulness, God does not lie in his promises, and therefore can be trusted in confidence with all our hearts. The bible says;

> God is not a man that he should lie
> Neither the son of man that he should repent:
> Hath he said, and shall he not do it?
> Or hath he spoken, and shall he not make it good?
> Numbers 23:19
> (2 Corinthians 1:20; Hebrews 6:17-18; Romans 3:3-4; Titus 1:2)

Why is it so important to know God the Father, especially in his faithfulness? It is to help our faith, trust and confidence in him. It is also to help us to believe in his word and promises. It is to enable us to build a covenantal relationship with him, as to whom and what he is: A faithful God.

We don't just have to know God as a faithful God and deal otherwise with him. As believers, we should also learn to go to him as a faithful God and pray to him as a faithful God, committing all that concerns us unto him as a faithful God. Not only that, we should also expect to receive from him as a faithful God; just as we see him as a loving, merciful, gracious and a just God. If we can lift our faith and come to this realm of relationship with the Father, miracles, signs and wonders which are already made as part of our lives in Christ; will begin to manifest in our everyday lives. We will not only be partakers of his divine nature; we will also experience the divine nature of which He has made us partakers, (2 Peter 1:4). The apostle Peter encourages us in this way,

> Wherefore let them that suffer according
> To the will of God, commit the keeping of their souls
> To him in well doing (or good works)

> As unto a faithful Creator (God)
> 1 Peter 4:19

Our God can be trusted. He is forever faithful… and his faithfulness cannot be compared to anything that the mind and the imagination of man can reach out to. And the apostle Paul in talking about the faithfulness of God simply put it this way that even;

> If we believe not, yet he abideth faithful
> He cannot deny himself
> 2 Timothy 2:13

And if the great I AM cannot deny himself of being faithful, who else in heaven, on earth and under the earth can!

IN CONCLUSION

Treasures and rewards are also translated as crowns in the word of God and it is good to know that the ones that are laid up for ourselves in heaven are not there for us only after we leave this world to go be with the Lord in heaven. We can begin to enjoy them right from here on earth. But enjoying the treasures we lay up in heaven does not end only here on earth. The enjoyment of the treasures continues also in heaven where we go be with the Lord and are received in crowns of glory (1 Peter 5:4). And there are of course many crowns but for the sake of time and space, we may not be able to go into their details. However, these crowns include some of the following;

The Crown of Rejoicing and this is for them that have won others to faith in Jesus Christ. (1 Thessalonians 2:19).

The Crown of Righteousness and this is also for all believers who long for the return of Christ (2 Timothy 4:8)

The incorruptible Crown which is for victorious life of purity in Christ (1 Corinthians 9:25)

The Crown of life which I believe is a dedicated one for all Christians that die as martyrs in Christ because of their faith in Christ (Revelation 2:10)

Now because of our direct or indirect connection with heaven, our treasures laid up in heaven can already be accessed and tapped into for use and enjoy right here on earth if we are in Christ. It can also be tapped into for use right here on the earth if Jehovah the great I am, the God of all creation and the living God is also your God and your Father (John 20:17); the source of your sufficiency and your supply (2 Corinthians 3:4-5)

Perhaps many may not know that once we come to be in Christ the whole resources of God and heaven becomes open unto us to enjoy and rejoice in them. The God of all creation becomes our God and our Father, he becomes our very provider and source of supply for all things and everything according to the riches of his glory which is in Christ Jesus (2 Corinthians 5:17-18; Philippians 4:19). It is in combination with all the resources of heaven made available at our disposal and our personal life of righteousness, based on faith in Christ on this earth that we lay treasures for ourselves in heaven. It becomes more important to know then what these resources are, which are only found in Christ Jesus. All of these heavenly resources of God's blessings, promises, inheritance, favour, and prosperity for us to live by on this earth, are in Christ (Ephesians 1:3) and they are kept for us in heaven (1 Peter 1:4) or the heavenly places where the bible reveals that, we have been made by God the Father to sit in Christ (Ephesians 2:6). Besides, they are of God the Father; but they are in Christ Jesus. And because they are in Christ Jesus, it means that we can only access them in and through our Lord and Saviour Jesus Christ by faith (Ephesians 2:18; Romans 5:1-2)

If these resources by which we need to live in order to lay up treasures for ourselves in heaven are of God and kept for us in heaven, then they will have to come down to us from heaven; or that we would have to go up to heaven for them. This is what I call as a divine connection which is only made possible by the Spirit of God in us through prayer (Romans 8:26-28; 1 Corinthians 2:9-12).

Again the bible reveals that in Christ Jesus, we have become God's children by a divine adoption whereby God has given us the spirit of adoption and sonship. By the spirit of adoption and sonship, we are able to call him our God and our Father. In this case the bible says that we have become heirs of God and joint-heirs with Christ. What belongs to God belongs to us all his resources have been made available unto us. We live in him and through him by his Son Jesus Christ. And in him, the bible says that we move and contain our being since our life is hid with Christ in God (Colossians 3:3-4)

So our Lord Jesus Christ in teaching us how to connect to the heavens or the heavenly places, and how to connect to the Father in heaven through prayer; taught us to ask for the Father's will to be revealed and done in the situations and circumstances of our lives in Christ right here on earth.

As we connect to the heavens or the heavenly places by the Holy Spirit who abides in us, God the Father reveals unto us from heaven what we have need of to do in order to have our spiritual blessings and inheritance manifested in the natural, material and financial world. We should remember that all of these are done in faith according to the word and promises of God the Father concerning his blessings, inheritance, favour and prosperity for us in and through Christ (Philippians 4:19)

Thus we access the heavens and the throne room for God's spiritual blessings and inheritance for us in Christ. Thus we access our heavenly or divine account in the heavenly places by faith; all right here on earth. So therefore, it does not necessarily mean that we have to go be with the Lord before we can begin to enjoy from our heavenly account as far as the treasures we have laid up for ourselves in heaven is concerned. This is not the plan of God the Father, and it has never been and shall never be his plan for us. Rather, his plan is that we would enjoy from our heavenly account right here on earth. That is why he pronounced his blessings upon us (Genesis 1:26-31; Ephesians 1:3); and the bible says that his blessings are upon us to make us rich (Psalm 3:8; Proverbs 10:6, 22). And also for us to live in the abundance and overflow of life right here on earth and in this world but in Christ. It is the more reason why being in Christ is very important in order to be able to lay up treasures for yourself in heaven and also to be able to access and enjoy out of your heavenly account especially if you are a Believer. And for those who are not believers in Christ, they will have a need of him as their Lord and Savior by asking him into their heart before they can access the good things of God for them. Because with all the promises, blessings, favour, inheritance and prosperity of the Father for us in him, Christ becomes the portal or the entrance into accessing these good things stored or laid up for us in our heavenly account. We should learn to take note that this heavenly account is not like the natural sense of a bank account on earth where money is the contents.

However though, everything that we do in kind or cash based on the will of the Father concerning salvation also accredits our heavenly accounts from which we are also able to draw our rewards of grace, love, peace, joy etc, from God the Father. A most important thing in connection with laying up treasures for ourselves in heaven is the heart matter in the application of all that God has for us in Christ.

Now the heavenly account holds all the riches of God for us in Christ. By these riches we live on earth and in this world to lay up for ourselves treasures in heaven. In other words, everything which is needed to lay up treasures in heaven does not depend on this natural world but they should be of God and from God. It should be by his ways. It should be by his plans and it should be by his purposes according to his will. Therefore, laying up treasures for ourselves in heaven involves also the use of our God-given life, time and resources of God for us in Christ. It is also the use of divine gifts and talents, both spiritual and natural of God for us in Christ and how all of these are combined in the will of God to bring glory to him.

It is only when we know and understand the promises, blessings and inheritance of god for us and how they are credited to our heavenly account, that we would also know and understand how to withdraw from them by faith. And withdrawals are not limited but as much as you can handle according to the Father's will to bring glory unto him by being rich towards heaven. After all this is why treasures are laid up for ourselves in heaven. Hence our Lord tells us;

>Lay not up for yourselves treasures upon earth
>Where moth and rust doth corrupt
>And where thieves break through and steal
>But lay up for yourselves treasures in heaven
>Where neither moth nor rust doth corrupt
>And where thieves do not break through nor steal
>For where your treasure is
>There will your heart be also
>Matthew 6:19-21

And then again

>Labour not for the meat which perisheth
>But for that meat which endureth unto everlasting life
>Which the Son of man shall give unto you
>For him has God the Father sealed
>John 6:27
>(Isaiah 55:2)

To God be the glory

www.ingramcontent.com/pod-product-compliance
Lightning Source LLC
Chambersburg PA
CBHW021153080526
44588CB00008B/315